D0475554

A BRIDGE TO THE FUTURE

Rama IX Bridge, built in 1987 on the occasion of the auspicious
60th birthday of His Majesty King Bhumibol Adulyadej The Great,
whose dedication, benevolence and wisdom have given the Thai
people hope for a better future.

Fog cloaks the ridges of Doi Inthanon National Park southwest of Chiang Mai. **GALEN ROWELL**

MAJOR SUPPORT FOR A DAY IN THE LIFE OF THAILAND WAS PROVIDED BY:

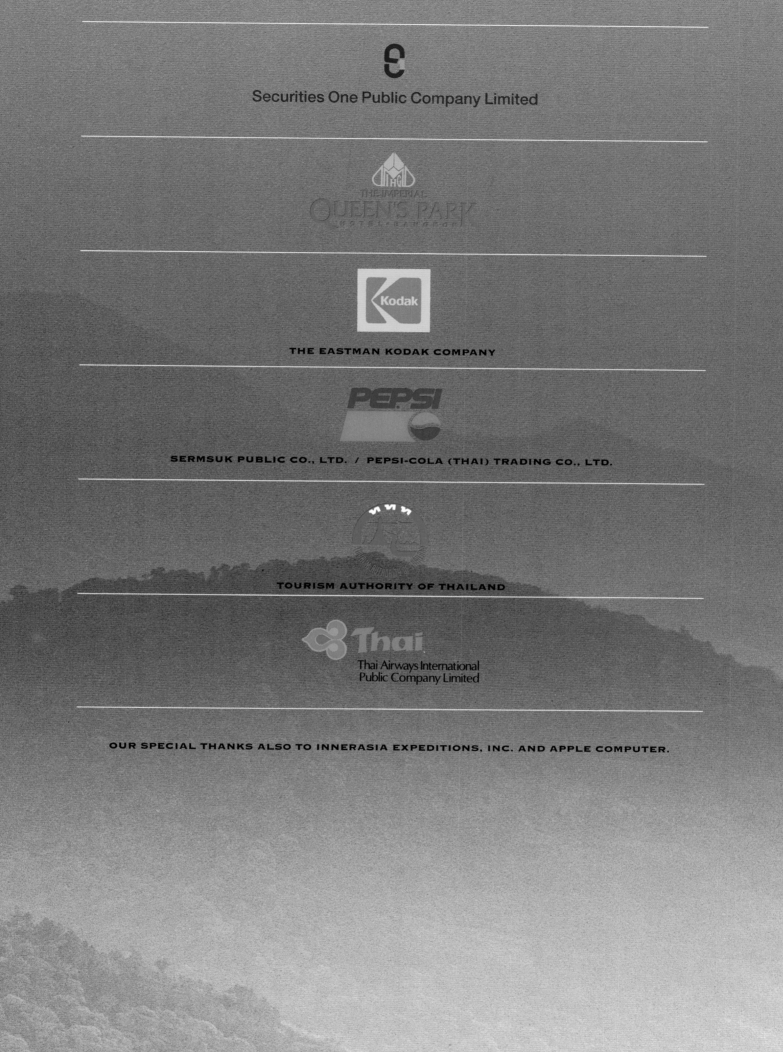

Securities One Public Company Limited

THE EASTMAN KODAK COMPANY

SERMSUK PUBLIC CO., LTD. / PEPSI-COLA (THAI) TRADING CO., LTD.

TOURISM AUTHORITY OF THAILAND

Thai Airways International
Public Company Limited

OUR SPECIAL THANKS ALSO TO INNERASIA EXPEDITIONS, INC. AND APPLE COMPUTER.

A fisherman guards *hoi krong* (cockle) beds in the warm waters of
Phangnga Bay, north of Phuket.   JOHN EVERINGHAM

A Day in the Life of
THAILAND

DIRECTED AND EDITED BY
DAVID COHEN

PROJECT CO-DIRECTORS
RICK BROWNE
JAMES MARSHALL

DIRECTOR OF PHOTOGRAPHY
PETER HOWE

DESIGNED BY
TOM MORGAN

TEXT BY
SUSAN WELS AND STEVE VAN BEEK

CollinsPublishersSanFrancisco
A Division of HarperCollinsPublishers

The spired *chedis* of Wat Phra Sri Sanphet, built by King Trailokanart in the 15th century, rise among the ruined temples and palaces of Ayutthaya—a Buddhist kingdom that flourished on the central Thai plains for 400 years. Before it was sacked by the Burmese in 1767, the metropolis of Ayutthaya had more citizens than London and awed European visitors with its sumptuous art and culture.
NIK WHEELER

Tha Muang, in fertile Kanchanaburi province, is located in a valley watered by the Khwae Noi and Khwae Yai rivers. Here, a woman walls a rice paddy, preparing it for the winter crop. **FRANK FOURNIER**

A leafy canopy of rubber trees shades motorists on the tropical island of Phuket in southern Thailand. **PASCAL MAITRE**

First published in 1995 by Collins Publishers San Francisco.

Copyright © 1995 Collins Publishers San Francisco

*Library of Congress Cataloging-in-Publication Data
A day in the life of Thailand/ directed and edited by David Cohen; project co-
directors, Rick Browne, James Marshall; director of photography, Peter Howe;
designed by Tom Morgan; text by Susan Wels, Steve Van Beek.
    p. cm.
    ISBN: 0-00-255481-X
    I. Thailand—Pictorial works. I. Cohen, David, 1955-. II. Wels, Susan.
III. Van Beek, Steve, 1944-.
DS566.2.D39 1995
959.304'4'0222—dc20   94-43683
                                                       CIP

Design: Tom Morgan, Blue Design, San Francisco, California
Printed in Singapore

10 9 8 7 6 5 4 3 2 1

興 國
KUO HSIN
PANAMA

At busy Klong Toey port, incoming freighters wait as long as a week to berth. To ease the strain, a new container port has been built at Laem Chabang on the Gulf of Thailand, and more are planned. SUSAN MEISELAS

A Day in the Life of Thailand
Photographers and Their Assigned Locations

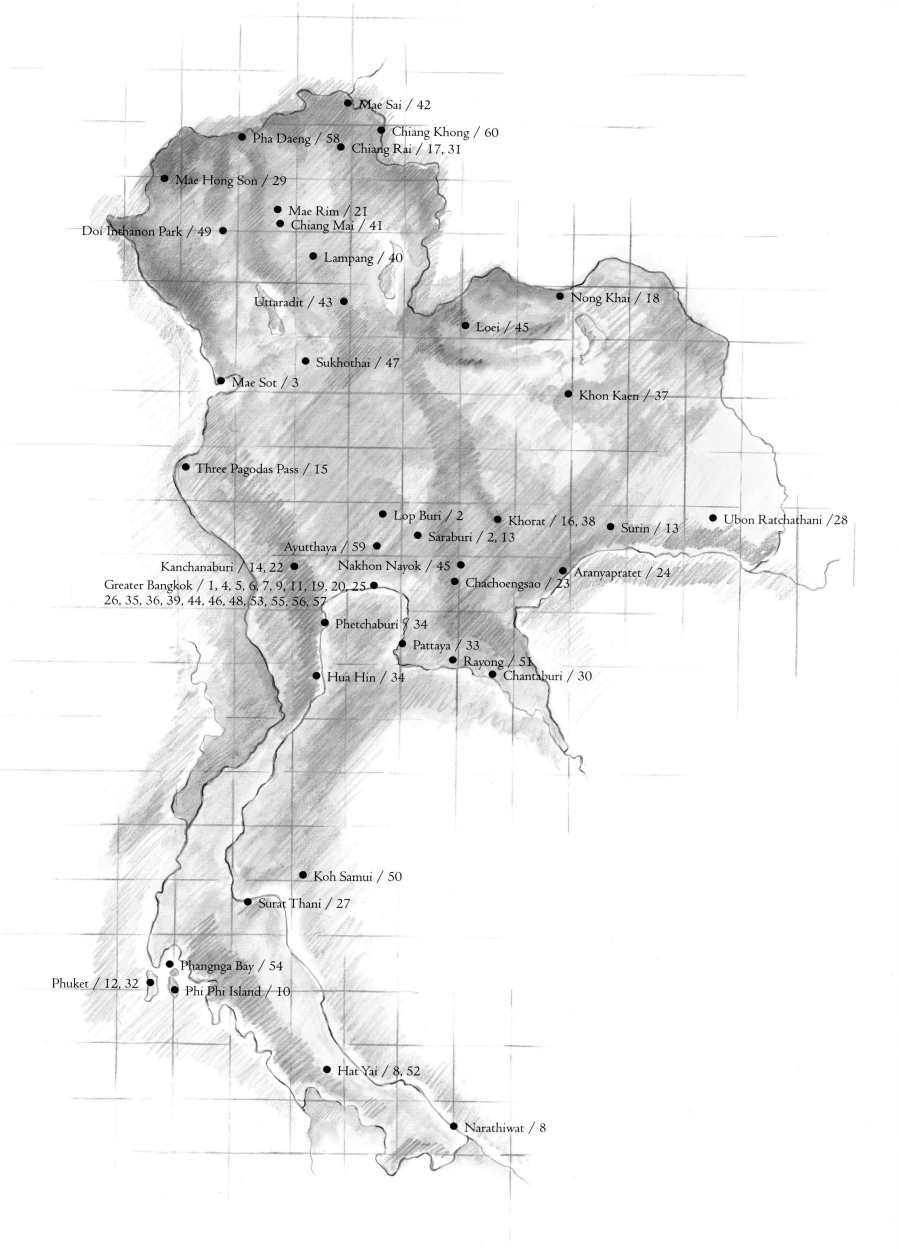

Mae Sai / 42

Chiang Khong / 60

Pha Daeng / 58

Chiang Rai / 17, 31

Mae Hong Son / 29

Mae Rim / 21

Chiang Mai / 41

Doi Inthanon Park / 49

Lampang / 40

Nong Khai / 18

Uttaradit / 43

Loei / 45

Sukhothai / 47

Khon Kaen / 37

Mae Sot / 3

Three Pagodas Pass / 15

Lop Buri / 2

Khorat / 16, 38

Surin / 13

Ubon Ratchathani / 28

Saraburi / 2, 13

Ayutthaya / 59

Nakhon Nayok / 45

Kanchanaburi / 14, 22

Aranyapratet / 24

Greater Bangkok / 1, 4, 5, 6, 7, 9, 11, 19, 20, 25
26, 35, 36, 39, 44, 46, 48, 53, 55, 56, 57

Chachoengsao / 23

Phetchaburi / 34

Pattaya / 33

Rayong / 51

Hua Hin / 34

Chantaburi / 30

Koh Samui / 50

Surat Thani / 27

Phangnga Bay / 54

Phuket / 12, 32

Phi Phi Island / 10

Hat Yai / 8, 52

Narathiwat / 8

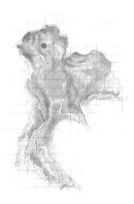

● **LEFT:**

Aᴺ orange vendor dozes before dawn in Chiang Mai, Thailand's second largest city. Until the Bangkok-Chiang Mai railway line was completed in the 1920s, thick jungle and mountainous terrain kept the city largely isolated. Now, however, good roads and frequent air service have made Chiang Mai an important commercial center for regional handicrafts and crops from the northern valleys.

ROBIN MOYER

● **RIGHT:**

Sprays of fresh orchids—purchased as everyday gifts and temple offerings—brighten a street stall on Bangkok's busy Sukhumvit Road. Thai orchids are flown overnight from Bangkok to flower markets throughout Europe.

SCOTT THODE

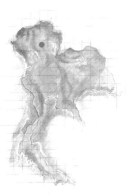

An elephant enjoys his morning bath at the Young Elephants Training Center near Lampang in northern Thailand. Even more than horses in Western cultures, elephants have always played a special role in Thailand, serving as cavalry mounts and high-capacity lumber haulers. The elephant training center was originally founded to teach young elephants to perform practical logging tasks. Since the government banned logging in 1989, however, the center has functioned increasingly as a tourist attraction. There were hundreds of thousands of elephants in Thailand a century ago, but due to deforestation, the elephant population has dwindled to fewer than 5,000.

CLAUS MEYER

● **RIGHT:**

Camping in *glots*—small tents hung from their umbrellas— 9,000 monks from all over Thailand gather for the Buddhist festival of Makha Puja on the grounds of Wat Dhammakai, 30 miles (50 kilometers) outside of Bangkok. Makha Puja commemorates the spontaneous gathering, 2,500 years ago, of 1,250 enlightened monks to hear the Buddha preach.

KRAIPIT PHANVUT

● **FOLLOWING PAGES:**

Until this century, rivers and canals were the highways and byways of Thailand's flood-prone central valley, where monsoon rains can turn streets into waist-deep streams. Although many canals have been filled to create roads, some—like Klong Damnoen Saduak in Ratchaburi province, southwest of Bangkok—still serve as watery thoroughfares. Here, vendors hawk their goods at floating markets; parents speed kids to school in noisy motorboats, and saffron-robed monks paddle door-to-door to receive their morning alms.

JAMES MARSHALL

For Thai Buddhists, the ritual of *bintabat*—giving morning alms to monks—is a daily opportunity to gain spiritual merit. Supplicants offer monks the first portion of the morning meal, receiving a blessing in return. This food provides the monks' only sustenance for the entire day. In a small village, a little girl places an offering in a monk's alms bowl, being careful not to touch any part of his body or his robes.

DILIP MEHTA

● **ABOVE:**

Morning *tai chi chuan* exercises in Bangkok's lovely Queen Sirikit Park on Sukhumvit Road.

PAUL CHESLEY

● **RIGHT:**

Motorcycles are often the only reliable way of moving through the congested streets of Bangkok, where rush hour traffic creeps along at a stately 2.5 miles (4 kilometers) per hour. To get their children to school on time, many parents resort to driving off with their sleeping children at 4 a.m., feeding and dressing them upon arrival.

PAUL CHESLEY

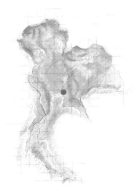

● **LEFT:**

At Wat Ratchaburana in Bangkok, a monk leads students from the Suksanaree Girls School in prayer while circling the temple three times. This is a traditional form of worship during Buddhist festivals.

PASSAKORN PAVILAI

● **ABOVE:**

A worshipper studies the Koran at the Haroon mosque in Bangkok, one of 2,000 Islamic temples in the kingdom. More than two million Moslems, most of Malay ancestry, comprise the largest religious minority in predominantly Buddhist Thailand. Thai Moslems enjoy full religious freedom, with 200 state-supported religious schools and, in some areas, government-sanctioned religious courts that adjudicate disputes according to Koranic law.

ABBAS

● ABOVE:

A Moslem student wearing the traditional *hiyap* (Islamic headcovering) pores over her books at Chulalongkorn University in Bangkok. Thailand's first university, Chulalongkorn was founded in 1917 by King Vajiravudh (Rama VI), and named for his father. Chulalongkorn is one of 42 state-run and private universities in Thailand.

SOMCHAI SATAYAPITAK

● RIGHT:

W riting and arithmetic lessons begin the day at the Chonnabot village elementary school in northeast Thailand.

JOSEPH MCNALLY

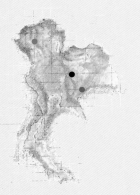

● At the Sri Aranyothai Primary School in Aranyaprathet, near the Cambodian border, the day's vocabulary words include *magic, democracy, benevolent* and *Buddha*. As a result of compulsory education laws, Thailand's literacy rate has risen to more than 91 percent. **ED KASHI**

● Students at the Phuttisophol Primary School in Chiang Mai assemble for the Thai national anthem, broadcast throughout the kingdom every day at 8 a.m. and 6 p.m. **ROBIN MOYER**

● Second-graders in *Luuk Sua Chao Baan* (The Wild Tiger Corps) wear their uniforms to school in Chonnabot, in Khon Kaen province.
JOE MCNALLY

● Two boys in the Blue Hmong hill tribe village of Nong Hoi work on a classroom exercise at Chomaelang Uppatam II school. Although Hmong children still maintain tribal customs, they are rapidly being assimilated into mainstream Thai society. **LINDSAY HEBBERD**

● **RIGHT:**

In a school yard in Nong Ki, near Nakhon Ratchasima in eastern Thailand, boys play an acrobatic match of net *takraw*—a national sport resembling volleyball, but played without hands. A net separates two teams of three players each. The players kick a hollow rattan or plastic ball back and forth, keeping it aloft with amazingly agile foot and elbow spikes, head butts and airborne somersaults. A more traditional version of takraw is played by six players standing in a circle.

Takraw buang (basket takraw) is another popular Thai sport that resembles basketball. A six-man team kicks the ball back and forth in a circle until one player propels the ball into a basket or ring hung 20 feet (6.5 meters) above the ground. The only traditional Thai sport involving a ball, takraw is played virtually every day in school yards, parks and temple courtyards throughout Thailand.

NEIL FARRIN

● **PREVIOUS PAGES:**

At Chonprathan Songkro elementary school in Nonthaburi, students line up for the national anthem.

STEVE HART

● **ABOVE:**
Monks at Wat Wachiralongkorn
near Nakhon Ratchasima
shave each other's heads in preparation
for the Makha Puja festival.

DILIP MEHTA

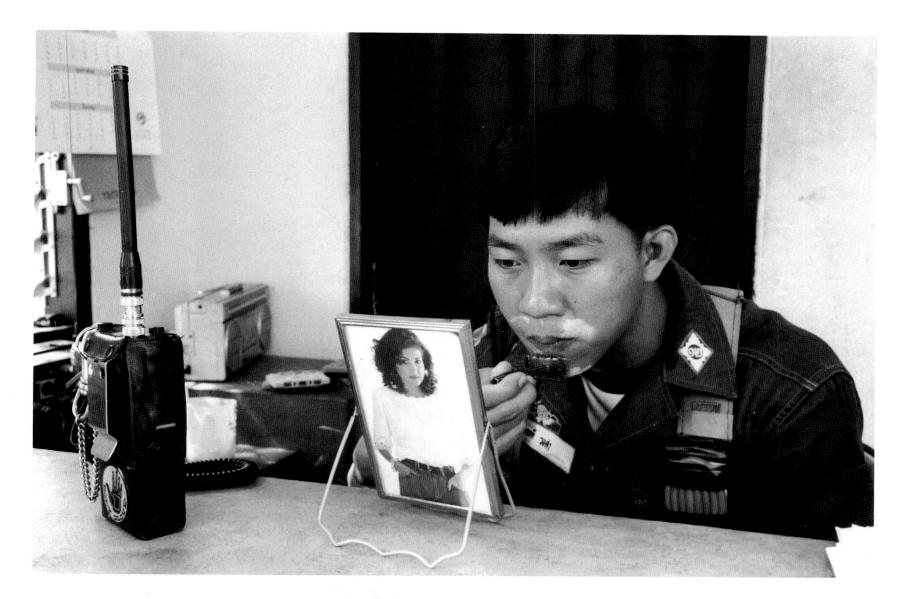

● **ABOVE:**

Rakkiaet Wongsa, 27, a Thai border policeman, shaves at his post at Aranyaprathet on the Cambodian frontier. Border guards in this area intercept smugglers crossing into Thailand. The woman pictured on the back of Khun Rakkiaet's mirror is a popular Thai movie star.

ED KASHI

● **FOLLOWING PAGES:**

Bangkok's Hualampong Station is the hectic hub of Thailand's efficient rail system. Scores of trains depart each day and night along three main lines. Passengers travel north to Chiang Mai, east to Ubon and south as far as Malaysia. Hualampong is also the point of entry for thousands of rural Thais seeking employment in the capital. Many spend their first night in Bangkok sleeping on the station's front lawn.

BRUNO BARBEY

Time	Destination (Thai)	Destination (English)	Platform
18.30	อุบลราชธานี	NONG KHAI	11
18.45	หนองคาย	AYUTTHAYA	10
19.00	อยุธยา •	NAKHON SITHAMMARAT	7
19.10	นครศรีธรรมราช	CHIANG MAI	5
19.20	เชียงใหม่	NAKHON SITHAMMARAT	9
19.40	นครศรีธรรมราช	DEN CHAI	6
19.45	เด่นชัย	PHITSANULOK	4
20.00	พิษณุโลก	NONG KHAI	10
20.10	หนองคาย	UDON TANI	8
20.30	อุดรธานี	UBON RATCHATHANI	7
20.40	อุบลราชธานี	SURIN	4
21.00	สุรินทร์	CHIANG MAI	10
21.50	เชียงใหม่	SURAT THANI	9
22.00	สุราษฎร์ธานี	UBON RATCHATHANI	5
22.35	อุบลราชธานี	PHITSANULOK	8
22.45	พิษณุโลก	UBON RATCHATHANI	
23.10	อุบลราชธานี		
23.25			

NO SERVICE ON SATURDAY

● RIGHT:

tooping over a flooded paddy near Sukhothai in central Thailand, a woman plants rice seedlings. For over 700 years, the Thai people have been cultivating rice in the fertile central plains. In the 13th century, the Thais founded their first independent kingdom, Sukhothai, in the rich, rice-growing land of the Chao Phya basin.

LARRY PRICE

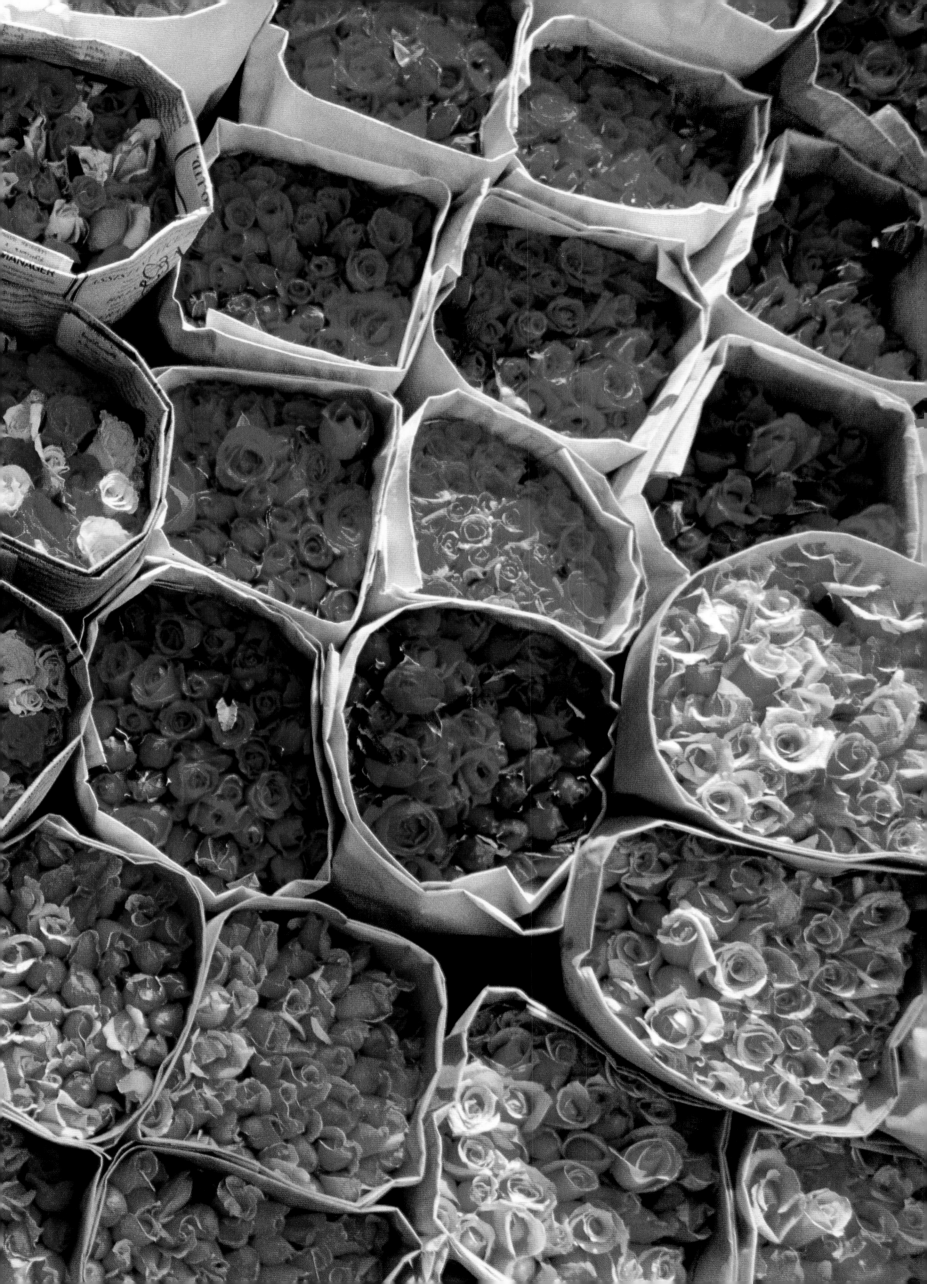

A DAY IN THE LIFE OF AN EXECUTIVE
BY JAY BRADLEY

Sumontip Otrakul, first vice president of Thai Farmers Bank, attends a briefing on the bank's new computer software system.

In the 18th century, two Thai sisters, Chan and Muk, became national heroes when they disguised themselves as male warriors and led the forces that expelled the Burmese from Phuket. In the late 20th century, women have taken leadership roles throughout Thai society. In 1983, the first woman *phu-yai-ban* (village headman) was elected, and the first female provincial governor was named in 1993. As a result of a 1974 constitutional amendment, the King may now be succeeded by a royal daughter—breaking a 700-year tradition of male succession to the throne.

As Thailand's economy expands, increased demand for well-educated workers has also led to expanded opportunities for women. *Day in the Life* photographer Jay Bradley spent a day with Sumontip Otrakul, first vice president of Thai Farmers Bank, as she juggled her responsibilities at home and on the job.

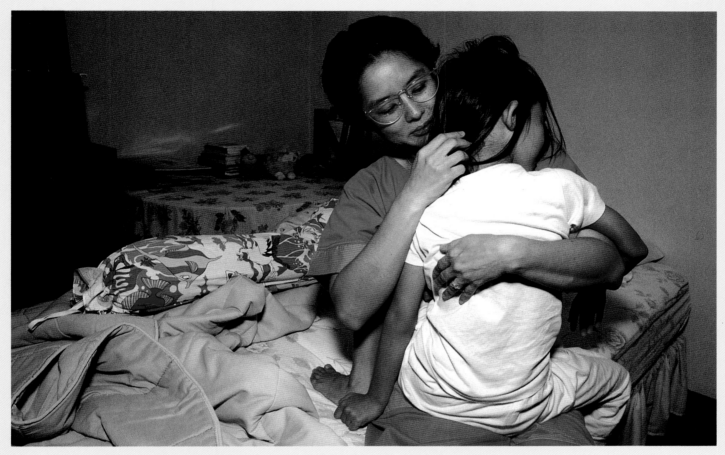

Rousing sleepy six-year-old, Pui, with a hug, Sumontip begins her day at 5:30 a.m. She must get her two daughters dressed, fed and to school by 8 a.m. In Bangkok traffic, the trip to school takes more than an hour.

Before setting off to school with a private car and driver, Pui and Pum bow to their mother and honor her with a *wai*, the Thai gesture of respect. Like all Thai children, Khun Sumontip's children are called by their nicknames. Pui's real name is Worasumon; Pum's is Worathip.

Khun Sumontip reviews potential changes in Thai Farmer's Bank's communications network with Phongthawat Phuankanok, first vice president of the bank's computer department.

A quick look out the window confirms that afternoon traffic is already backing up on Bangkok's streets—a sure sign Khun Sumontip's children will have a long ride home from school.

Arriving home at 5:45 p.m., Khun Sumontip prepares the family's dinner.

Looking up from her to-do list, she smiles at Pui and her husband, Weearwudht Otrakul, who owns an architectural firm in Bangkok.

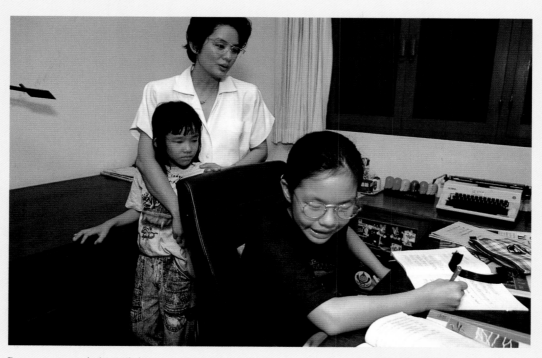

Pum gets some help with homework before bedtime.

● **LEFT:**

An Akha mother and child pose for photographer Barry Lewis in Gui Satai, a hill tribe village in the northern mountains near Mae Chan. Thailand's 25,000-plus Akha are originally from southern China. Once nomadic opium growers, they have now settled in permanent villages established by the Thai government. There, the Akha have adapted modern cultivation techniques instead of the slash-and-burn form of agriculture that once contributed to Thailand's rapid deforestation. The Akha now cultivate rice, which they regard as a sentient being requiring elaborate propitiation ceremonies. Akha headdresses are usually adorned with pre-1947 silver coins issued by the British Raj in India.

BARRY LEWIS

● **ABOVE:**

A shy Hmong (*Meo*) child clings to his mother in Chiang Khong village in northern Thailand. White Hmong women wear small embroidered caps and black skirts, while Blue Hmong women wear their hair in large buns and dress in skirts covered with embroidery.

LINDSAY HEBBERD

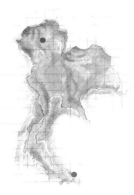

● **LEFT:**
These women of the Padawn Karen hill tribe are refugees from Myanmar. Among the last of the "long-necked women," they live in the village of Ban Nai Soi, west of Chiang Mai. The traditional brass rings appear to stretch the women's necks but, in fact, depress their collarbones.
DANIEL LAINÉ

● **FOLLOWING PAGES:**
A fishing boat painted in a traditional Moslem design in Narathiwat on the Gulf of Thailand.
RICK BROWNE

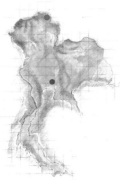

● **RIGHT:**

Prapansak Bhatayanond, general manager of Bangkok's luxurious Imperial Queen's Park Hotel, displays the hotel's prize attraction—the largest penthouse suite in all of Asia. The palatial, 8,000-square-foot (750-square-meter) apartment features three bedrooms, a reception hall, dining room, living room, sauna, private fitness room, study, four bathrooms and a full-service kitchen, as well as an outdoor jacuzzi and panoramic views. It's all available for $4,000 a night, including the services of two butlers.

JAMES MARSHALL

● **FOLLOWING PAGES:**

The seasonal cycles of rice planting and harvesting shape the rhythm of Thai life. The kingdom is the world's largest exporter of rice, and more than half its population is involved in growing, processing, transporting and marketing the grain. In the northern village of Mae Chan, workers at the Poon Jar Bon rice mill dry *khao suai*, a premium-grade white rice, before taking it to market.

BARRY LEWIS

● RIGHT:

Silk weaving, a 6,000-year-old industry in Asia, is practiced by more than 300,000 families in Thailand, particularly in the north-eastern provinces. Thai silk, first popularized around the world in the late 1950s by American Jim Thompson, is known for its nubby texture and brilliant, iridescent colors. In Thai silk-weaving villages such as Chonnabot in Khon Kaen province, families raise silkworms in their homes, boiling the cocoons to release raw silk threads. In a culture where almost nothing is wasted, silkworms are often sprinkled with salt or curried and eaten as snacks.

JOSEPH MCNALLY

● FOLLOWING PAGES:

The infamous "bridge over the River Khwai" spans the Meklong (Khwai Yai) River a few miles outside the town of Kanchanaburi. Only the end sections remain from the original bridge—part of the 230-mile (370-kilometer) "Death Railway" built by Allied and Asian prisoners during World War II. The line—linking Bangkok and Burma through nearly impenetrable jungle and mountain terrain—was to supply troops for the proposed Japanese invasion of India. More than 180,000 Asians and 60,000 Allied soldiers worked as slaves under ghastly conditions, and more than 90,000 perished in the process. The bridge was used only once by the Japanese before it was destroyed by Allied bombers in February 1945.

ROBERT HOLMES

A Day in the Life of a Rubber Plantation

BY PASCAL MAITRE

A Phuket rubber tapper starts work before dawn, wearing a calcium carbide headlamp.

Inland from the quiet coves and resort beaches of Phuket Island, hundreds of Thai families operate small rubber plantations. These small holdings are among the nearly 800,000 family-run latex farms in Thailand's 14 southern provinces. Together, these plantations cultivate, collect and process enough natural rubber to make Thailand the world's leading producer and exporter.

First introduced to Thailand 100 years ago, rubber trees thrive in the rain-soaked South. Harvesting and processing their valuable sap is a laborious process that begins each day in the cool pre-dawn hours. Despite a shortage of farm labor in the rapidly developing southern provinces, Thailand's rubber production has been growing at a robust 10 percent a year.

Atapper slashes open a wound in the bark of a rubber tree to release the flow of latex.

Most of Thailand's original rubber trees (*hevea braziliensis*) have been replaced with high-yield hybrids that produce latex only six years after planting. To earn income while the groves mature, some families plant cashews or pineapples between their rows of young rubber trees.

ABOVE AND BELOW: Once the latex has been collected, tappers carry it in buckets to a processing shed, where it is poured into pans and mixed with chemicals. After the latex has solidified, it is fed through a mangle which stretches, softens and grooves the rubber. The latex sheets are dried in the sun for five days or cured in a smokehouse before being sold to markets in Japan, China and the United States.

In Phuket, and throughout southern Thailand, rubber workers are being lured off the farms by higher wages offered in the rapidly expanding building and transportation industries. Rubber workers earn about 50 baht ($2) per day, compared to the 100 baht daily wage paid at construction sites.

● **ABOVE:**

In the dusty northeastern village of Chonnabot, a stud pig is chauffeured to a well-paying rendezvous.

JOE MCNALLY

● **RIGHT:**

No elephants allowed" is the rule—but not necessarily the reality—in downtown Surin, a provincial capital in eastern Thailand. A quiet town most of the year, Surin attracts hordes of tourists in late November, when the annual Elephant Roundup—a hugely popular three-day rodeo—is held in Surin Sports Park. Forty thousand spectators watch more than 200 astonishingly agile elephants dance, play soccer, run races, roll logs and stage mock battles. The elephants are trained by the Suay tribe (Thai Kuy), who speak to their charges in a Khmer dialect.

NEIL FARRIN

● **RIGHT:**

Ranks of shrink-wrapped Buddhas stand ready for sale outside Charoenchai Karnchang Buddhist Supplies in Bangkok.

SCOTT THODE

● **FOLLOWING PAGES:**

A gardener tends the Kanchanaburi War Cemetery, a memorial for some of the thousands of Allied prisoners of war who died while building the infamous Death Railway between Thailand and Burma during World War II. The soldiers' names, ranks and brief epitaphs are recorded on rows of solemn markers.

ROBERT HOLMES

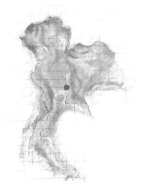
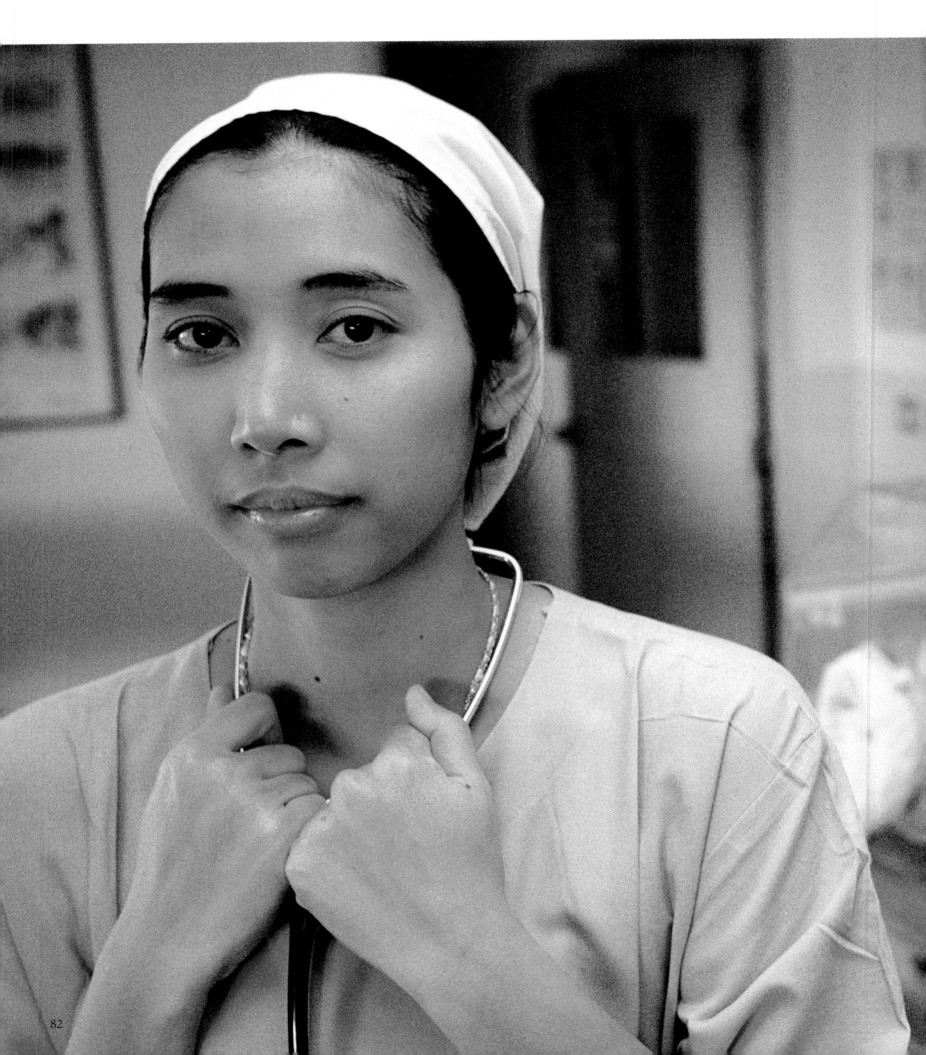

● LEFT:

A nurse watches over premature babies in the intensive care nursery of Bangkok Christian Hospital. In Bangkok and other urban areas, traditional Thai medicine combining herbal, massage and spiritual healing is practiced side-by-side with Western medicine. The latter was introduced to Thailand by the king's father, Prince Mahidol of Songkhla, who studied at Harvard Medical School.

DAVID ALAN HARVEY

● **RIGHT:**

At the Pholasith Motors factory outside Bangkok, a worker assembles *tuk-tuks*—Thailand's famous three-wheeled taxis. Tuk-tuks were originally named, onomatopo-etically, for the sputtering sound of their two-stroke engines. Although by the late 1970's these engines were replaced by quieter, natural-gas-powered motors, the name stuck.
ALEX WEBB

● **FOLLOWING PAGES:**

A monk scales a web of bamboo scaffolding around an unfinished Buddha image at Wat Sabon Kangthon in Saraburi province.
NEIL FARRIN

● **LEFT:**

Lush displays of Thai fruit beckon buyers at the Kanchanaburi market. The day's offerings include hairy red rambutans, sweet brown-fleshed langsat, ruby mangosteens, mangoes, grapes, papayas and juicy pepper-shaped *chompoos* (rose apples).

ROBERT HOLMES

● **ABOVE:**

In the off-season, working elephants and their keepers wander the streets of Bangkok inviting pregnant women to walk under the belly of the beast. The passage, which costs 20 baht (80 cents), is intended to bring good luck to unborn children. Between customers, this elephant begs for an extra treat from a sidewalk vendor.

PORNVILAI CARR

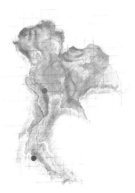

● ABOVE:

A *chao ley* (sea gypsy) spears a ray in the turquoise waters off Koh Phi Phi, southeast of Phuket. Island-hopping fishermen of Malay descent, chao ley rove the Andaman Sea from Burma to Malaysia. The Koh Phi Phi group of islands is home to thousands of chao ley.

PETER CHARLESWORTH

●RIGHT:

F amed throughout Thailand, *Mae Chi Loy Nam* ("the floating nun") meditates while floating supine in a pool of water at Wat Tham Mongkorn Thong, a Buddhist temple in Kanchanaburi. For an admission price of 20 baht (80 cents), visitors can enter the pool's amphitheater to receive the nun's silent blessings.

ROBERT HOLMES

● **LEFT:**

A live sea crab provides amusement for boys playing in the
waters off Koh Mak in Phangnga Bay.
JOHN EVERINGHAM

● **ABOVE:**

A hesitant tourist inspects a
poisonous Siamese Cobra at a
snake farm in Chiang Mai. Though
smaller and slightly less venomous
than the better-known King Cobras,
Siamese Cobras are more common and
equally deadly. A small group of men
make their living catching and selling
the snakes to leather dealers, street
vendors and Thailand's well-regarded
Saowapha Institute, which produces
anti-venom serum for rural clinics.

Street vendors concoct a different
sort of health potion. First, the
customer selects a live snake. Then, the
vendor slits the reptile's throat and
mixes its blood with cognac in a brandy
snifter. The customer quaffs the
mixture on the spot, and if he wishes,
takes the snake's gall bladder home to
eat later. The blood is thought to
strengthen one's constitution, while the
gall bladder is believed to improve
eyesight. This practice, deplored by
international wildlife organizations, is
discouraged by the Thai government.
CLAUS MEYER

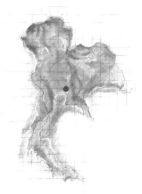

● LEFT:
Although many abandoned dogs and cats are given food and shelter at Buddhist temples throughout Thailand, these animals—some injured by speeding cars—are cared for at a private shelter on the outskirts of Bangkok. Run by a former kindergarten teacher and her husband, who works for the Ministry of Education, the animal refuge is supported by private donations.

JANE EVELYN ATWOOD

● ABOVE:
Tourists entrust their lives to the nimble feet and keen eyes of a performing pachyderm at the Crocodile Farm in Paknam, 18 miles (30 kilometers) southeast of Bangkok. The farm boasts the world's largest collection of crocodiles, including 30,000 Siamese specimens and varieties from as far away as the Amazon basin and the Nile River.

The farm was started by a Chinese leather dealer worried that overhunting of crocodiles would result in their extinction, denying him his supply of leather. It turned out he was right. The last Siamese crocodiles disappeared from the wild in the mid-1970s, and the species was preserved only because of the Crocodile Farm's collection.

SYLVIA PLACHY

A Day in the Life of a Country Studio

BY SHRIMP

Bangkok-based photographer Patrick Gauvain, widely known as "Shrimp," set up a roadside studio—à la Irving Penn—near the Myanmar (Burma) border at Three Pagodas Pass. In front of a white backdrop, Shrimp made portraits for an entire day. Many of the subjects were Burmese or members of the Mon and Karen tribes that live in the mountainous border regions. Shrimp has been chronicling Thai life—and photographing beautiful Thai women—since he first arrived in Southeast Asia in 1968.

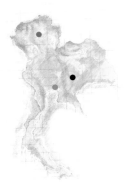

● **ABOVE:**

I n the impoverished neighborhood surrounding Bangkok's Klong Toey port, preschoolers stretch out for a midday nap at a primary school run by Kru Prateep Ungsongtham, known as "the slum angel." Since 1972, Kru Prateep's foundation has educated and cared for the neighborhood's needy children.

SUSAN MEISELAS

Tourists at Bangkok's Wat Phra Kaew, the Temple of the Emerald Buddha. The holiest shrine in Thailand, the temple adjoins the Grand Palace and contains a Buddha image that is actually made from jade, not emerald. Legend has it that the Emerald Buddha was discovered in the fifteenth century when lightning struck a *chedi* in the northern city of Chiang Rai. The precious icon was kept in various temples in the north before it was carried to Vientiane by plundering Laotians. King Rama I of Thailand conquered Vientiane in 1778 and brought the Emerald Buddha to Bangkok, where it has been enshrined, since 1784, in the royal Wat Phra Kaew.

A national symbol of freedom and prosperity, the Emerald Buddha is ritually garbed by the King of Thailand three times a year. In the cool season, the Buddha wears a robe of woven gold. In the hot season, it is covered with a diamond-studded gold tunic, and in the rainy season, it is draped with a saffron monk's robe.

NICK KELSH

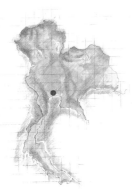

● **ABOVE:**

A special dress for a special occasion: a visit to a Bangkok amusement park.

PASSAKORN PAVILAI

● **PREVIOUS PAGES:**

Hair-raising fun at *Dan Naramit,* the popular "Magic Land" amusement park outside of Bangkok.

PASSAKORN PAVILAI

● **RIGHT:**

Father and son enjoy a day at Dusit Zoo in Bangkok. In modern Thailand—even in urban centers—family bonds remain remarkably strong. Children are not only cherished, but indulged.

NICK KELSH

● The headmistress and students of the Addinah School for Moslem girls in Bacho, near Narathiwat on Thailand's southern coast.
RICK BROWNE

● Band students in Chonnabot in Khon Kaen province blend the sounds of Thai and western instruments into the fast-paced melodies of *mo lam* and *luuk thung*—the country music of Isan. Although the popularity of classical Thai music has declined, pop and folk music from the northeastern provinces—especially songs about rural life and love—have a huge following throughout the country. Northeastern tunes are usually sung to the haunting, bagpipe-like tones of the *khaen*, a Laotian instrument comprised of a tall bundle of bamboo pipes. **JOE McNALLY**

● Soldiers relax near the Grand Palace in Bangkok. All 20-year-old Thai males are subject to two years of military service. Women are permitted to join the armed forces as volunteers. **PAUL CHESLEY**

● To raise money for building repairs, *wats* throughout Thailand hold glittery temple fairs featuring musical performances, outdoor movies, carnival rides and sideshows. This troupe of dancers from the Northeast is about to perform at the Wat Chakkawat fair in Bangkok.

PASSAKORN PAVILAI

● **ABOVE:**

Boys at the Wat Sra Kaew orphanage in Pa Mok, near Ayutthaya, line up for lunch—usually rice and curry. The 50-year-old temple orphanage—supported entirely by private donations—houses and educates 1,100 boys and girls from infancy through high school.

JANE EVELYN ATWOOD

● **ABOVE:**
Eleven-, twelve- and thirteen-year-old schoolgirls giggle in their seats at Wat Pochai in Nong Khai, before listening to a sermon. While Thai public schools are coeducational, most private schools are exclusively for boys or girls.
CAROL GUZY

● **ABOVE:**

Limestone monoliths jut from the Andaman Sea in Phangnga Bay. The most famous of these formations, Koh Tapu (Nail Island), was the setting for the 1973 James Bond thriller, *The Man with the Golden Gun*.

JOHN EVERINGHAM

● **RIGHT:**

Barges snake down the Chao Phya river, the grand river of kings that bisects Greater Bangkok into Bangkok proper (on the left) and Thonburi (on the right). The full Thai name for Bangkok is, according to *The Guinness Book of World Records*, the world's longest place name. It is Krungthep Mahanakhon Bovorn Rattanakosin Mahintharayutthaya Mahadilokpop Noparatratchathani Burirom Udomratchaniveymahasathan Amornpiman Avatarnsathit Sakkathattiya-avisnukarmprasit. In everyday usage, this is inevitably shortened to Krungthep, City of Angels.

PAUL CHESLEY

With the assistance and encouragement of the Thai government, Akha villagers in Pakheoy, near Mae Sai, have largely abandoned destructive slash-and-burn agriculture. Instead, they have settled in permanent bamboo and thatch houses to grow vegetables for sale in distant markets. When they are not farming, Akha men roam the hills near the Myanmar border, hunting birds and small game with barrel-loaded, single-shot long rifles.

BARRY LEWIS

A Buddhist Funeral

BY CAROL GUZY

ABOVE: A beautifully decorated wood-and-paper funerary tower—adorned with a picture of the deceased—contains a simple wood coffin.

LEFT: At the funeral of Pongsi Kaewsrengam in Nong Khai, the coffin is opened so relatives and friends can say their final good-byes. They anoint the corpse with lustral water before cremation.

In Buddhist doctrine, death is not the end of life, but rather a transition within a chain of lives. Each life, well lived, is another step toward nirvana, the end of suffering and desire. In Nong Khai, near the Laotian border, *Day in the Life* photographer Carol Guzy encountered a Buddhist funeral. The deceased was Pongsi Kaewsrengam, a 47-year-old mother of four who died after a long bout with cancer. Guzy was struck not only by the serenity of the mourners, but by their deep sense of community. Funerals in rural Thailand involve the entire village. Within these tightknit communities, everyone is known to everyone else, and each loss is a shared loss.

Relatives pray while monks chant prayers in Pali, the ancient Indian language of Thai Buddhism.

During three days and nights of mourning, friends and relatives gather at the home of the deceased. Few Thai occasions, no matter how solemn, remain grim for long. Friends not only console the family, but renew acquaintances, exchange gossip, watch movies and play cards.

Joined by a sacred white cord which transmits blessings, friends and relatives accompany Pongsi's coffin to the wat.

The pyre and coffin are set ablaze. The ashes and bones are traditionally retained by the family or ritually set afloat on a river.

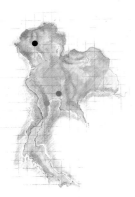

● PREVIOUS PAGES:

Wearing ceremonial clothing of coarse jute, mourners pray at the funeral of a relative at Wat Hualampong, a Chinese Buddhist (Mahayana) temple in central Bangkok. At the conclusion of the seven-day funeral ceremony, paper replicas of worldly goods such as Mercedes Benz automobiles and color televisions are burned. The smoke carries their essence to the afterlife for use by the deceased.

BRUNO BARBEY

● ABOVE:

Hilltops are generally reserved for religious monuments. The exception, pictured above, is the Wang Khao Wang summer palace. This complex was built by King Mongkut— Rama IV—who ruled Siam from 1851–68.

Set amid fragrant frangipani trees, the recently restored palace has large halls open to the breezes and superb views of Phetchaburi and the surrounding farmlands. Its most prominent structure is an old astronomical observatory. It was, in fact, his passion for astronomy that eventually led to the death of King Mongkut.

In 1868, the king predicted a full solar eclipse that could best be viewed from Pran Buri, south of Phetchaburi, and he transported a large contingent to the site. On the exact day and hour he had calculated, the sky darkened and the eclipse occurred. King Mongkut contracted an illness in Pran Buri and died one week later in Bangkok.

An odd version of King Mongkut's life is depicted in the famous Broadway musical and movie, *The King and I*. In a country where virtually all citizens regard their king with great reverence, *The King and I* is considered a nasty, insulting fabrication. All versions of the movie and play—and the book they are based on—are banned in Thailand.

JAMES MARSHALL

● RIGHT:

Buddhist monks at Vachiratharn Falls, a nearly 200-foot (65-meter) plunge over sheer granite cliffs halfway up Doi Inthanon, Thailand's tallest mountain.

GALEN ROWELL

● **LEFT:**

In Chiang Khong, a village on the Laotian border, a farmer hauls water from the Mekong River to irrigate his lettuce patch. As the river recedes during the dry season, farmers plant vegetable gardens in the rich alluvial soil.

MICHAEL YAMASHITA

● **PREVIOUS PAGES:**

Bangkok's modern shopping malls—air-conditioned palaces with car shows, food stands, ice-skating rinks and even rooftop amusement parks—are popular hangouts for shoppers and city teens.

PAUL CHESLEY

● **ABOVE:**

Until 1993—when the last of 370,000 Cambodian refugees left Thailand—Aranyaprathet was a crowded warren of refugee camps and international relief agencies. Now it is a main commercial gateway between Thailand and Cambodia. Cambodians willing to brave minefields and periodic skirmishes between the Thai army and the Khmer Rouge cross the border to trade fish and farm products for toothpaste, laundry soap, vehicles and other products that are scarce in Cambodia. Another class of traders offers Cambodian sapphires and rare woods from that country's rapidly disappearing forests.

ED KASHI

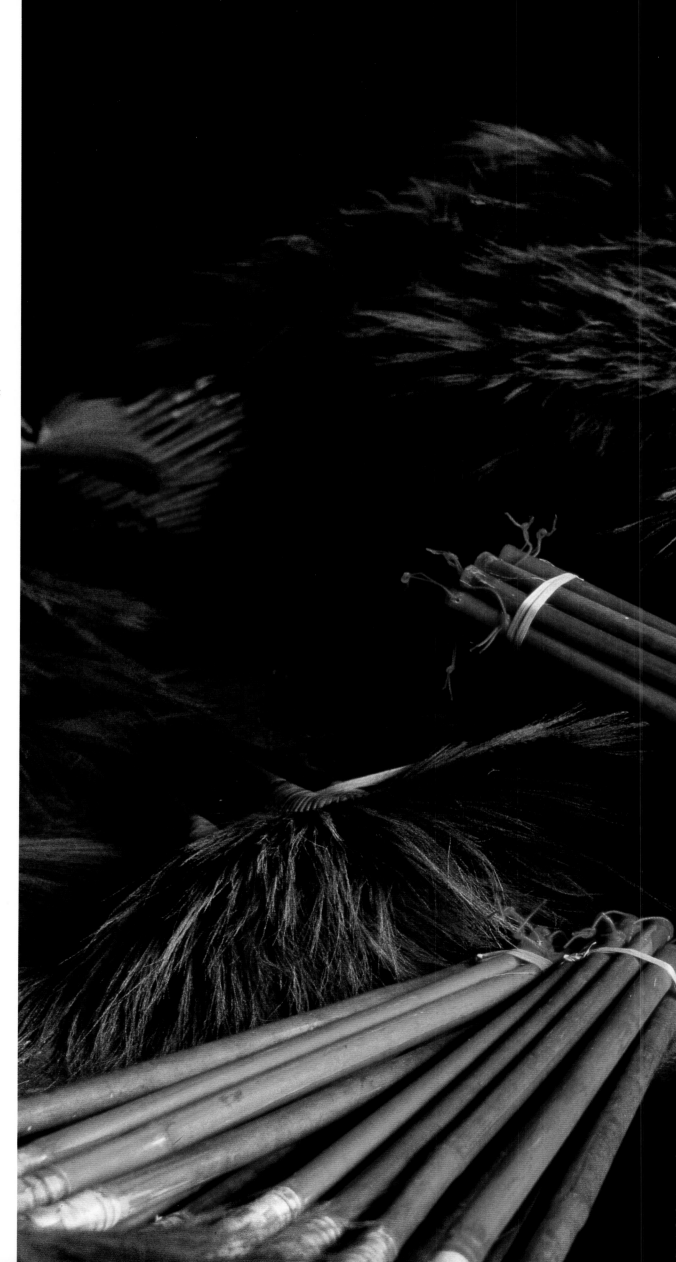

● **RIGHT:**

Throughout Thailand, cottage industries such as silk and basket weaving provide family income between agricultural seasons. In the cool, roomy space beneath a stilt-legged house in the village of Labrac, workers make traditional brooms using thin strips of bamboo to lash rush bristles to rattan handles.

BRIAN PALMER

Workers take a break at the Saha Union footwear factory in Chachoengsao. Employees of the Thai-owned plant produce internationally known brands of athletic shoes.

The Thai work force, steeped in a centuries-old craft tradition, performs detail work in a skillful fashion. Compared with local farmers, factory workers are well paid, but by western standards, employees work long hours (47-hour weeks) for a low wage (under $5 a day). These factors have made Thailand, traditionally an agricultural exporter, a leading exporter of manufactured goods as well.

CATHERINE KARNOW

Thailand, the only country in Asia that regularly exports more food than it imports, has developed a fast-growing processing industry for its abundant farm produce. In Mae Sot, on the western border with Myanmar, workers can fruits and vegetables at the Great Oriental Food Products Company.

JAN BANNING

Workers dash out the door as the 5 p.m. closing bell rings at the South East Wood Factory outside Rayong. Manufacturing plants on the rapidly developing eastern seaboard, provide employment for rural Thais who would otherwise look for work in Bangkok.

JEFFERY ALLAN SALTER

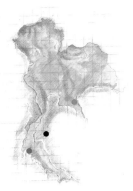

● RIGHT:

The interior of a towering
limestone rock in Phangnga Bay.
Many of these picturesque islands have
hollow, steeply-walled interiors open to
the sky. Some are inhabited by bands of
monkeys stranded over 10,000 years
ago when Ice Age glaciers retreated,
causing the world's oceans to rise by
several hundred feet.

JOHN EVERINGHAM

● LEFT:

Although most of the old ruby
and sapphire mines in
southeastern Thailand have been
nearly exhausted, workers continue to
pan for gems. In Bo Rai, east of
Chanthaburi, a laborer searches for
sapphires in the red mud of a strip
mine, placing any rough gems she
finds under her tongue.

SARAH LEEN

● ABOVE:

Since the first backpackers
arrived on a coconut boat in
1971, the island of Koh Samui has
been prized by foreign tourists as a
paradise of white sand, turquoise water
and tall palms. Located 52 miles (84
kilometers) southeast of Surat Thani
in the Gulf of Thailand, the island was
once a quiet coconut trading post.
Although tourism is now Koh Samui's
main business, islanders—assisted by
trained, tree-scaling macaque monkeys—still harvest and ship two
million coconuts a month.

STEVE RUBIN

A DAY IN THE LIFE OF THE KING AND QUEEN

BY KRAIPIT PHANVUT

I n 1955, King Bhumibol Adulyadej and Queen Sirikit became the first Thai rulers to visit the remote Northeast. The journey introduced them to the problems of rural Thais and inspired myriad programs to improve their conditions. The King is the longest-ruling monarch in Thai history. During his 49-year reign, he and the Queen have visited every province, reaching even the most inaccessible villages by helicopter, jeep, boat and foot. Together, the royal couple has initiated hundreds of projects to better the lives of the Thai people. A long-term program begun in the 1960s has helped wean hill tribes from their traditional dependence on opium cultivation. Other royal projects range from swamp drainage and water conservation to forest preservation and irrigation. *Day in the Life* photographer Kraipit Phanvut accompanied the King and the Queen on separate visits to the provinces.

● **ABOVE:** Her Majesty Queen Sirikit meets with villagers in a remote section of Loei Province on the Thai-Laotian border. One of the Queen's primary interests is working with rural women to develop sources of income, such as weaving and embroidery, to supplement farm revenues.

● **RIGHT:** In Ban Bung Khe, 72 miles (116 kilometers) northeast of Bangkok, His Majesty King Bhumibol Adulyadej meets with local officials to discuss plans for a new dam. The project is one of more than 1,000 environmental and economic development efforts in which the King has been personally involved.

● **LEFT:**

This eight-year-old *nak muay Thai* (Thai boxer) just won his fourth bout at a temple fair in the ancient Thai capital of Ayutthaya. Joining the ranks of Thailand's 60,000 full-time nak muay Thai fighters is a ticket to prosperity for many young boys, particularly those from the Northeast. Training in Thailand's most popular sport—which permits kicks, elbow jabs and knee thrusts as well as punches—can begin as early as age six or seven. Most boys start fighting for small purses in their early teens. This young boxer, cheered on by more than 200 spectators, beat a schoolmate in five two-minute rounds. In addition to the trophy, he took home a 300 baht ($12.00) purse, plus gifts of money from the ringside crowd.

NIK WHEELER

● **ABOVE:**

Private-school students practice social skills at a graduation party at Bangkok's Imperial Queen's Park Hotel.

DANIEL LAINÉ

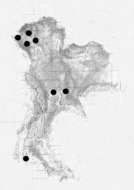

● A Malay woman at Koh Pannyi in Phangnga Bay.
JOHN EVERINGHAM

● In Chachoengsao, a large town 60 miles (100 kilometers) east of Bangkok, a young dancer waits to take her turn onstage at Wat Sothon Wararam Worawihaan. **CATHERINE KARNOW**

● The Padawn Karen tribe, refugees from Myanmar, once considered brass neck rings to be marks of beauty. The first rings were traditionally placed around a girl's neck at age five, and two new rings were added every second year. The practice is now in decline, and this girl now wears the rings only for tourists. **DANIEL LAINÉ**

● Thick scarves keep dust and sun off the faces of construction workers in Bangkok. **ABBAS**

● A Karen tribeswoman in Sop Hart, a mountain hill tribe village inside Doi Inthanon National Park. **GALEN ROWELL**

● A young Lahu Nyi (Red Lahu) woman in Pha Daeng is adorned for the hill tribe's raucous, eight-day New Year's celebration. Courtship is a highlight of the festival. Young men woo their wives-to-be by playing gourd flutes and teasing them with sticks through the bamboo slat floors of village huts. **NEVADA WIER**

● An orchid seller in Chiang Mai. **CLAUS MEYER**

● Draped with amulets to ensure health, prosperity, luck and potency, Boonrod Soitong, 62, lives with his nine-year-old daughter under the main highway between Bangkok and the border town of Trat. Since his house burned down during a Chinese New Year celebration 20 years ago, Soitong and his wife have raised five children beneath the overpass. **CATHERINE KARNOW**

● **LEFT:**

Mon Montri, a visiting 13-year-old novice, stands before the dazzling gold doors of Bangkok's Wat Phra Kaew, the only one of Thailand's 29,000 Buddhist temples in which no monks reside. Elaborate images of mythical *thawaraban* bar evil spirits from the shrine and protect the precious Emerald Buddha housed atop its golden altar.

NICK KELSH

● **ABOVE:**

Unlike the vast majority of ethnic Thais, who practice Theravada (Lesser Vehicle) Buddhism, many of Thailand's ethnic Chinese practice Mahayana (Greater Vehicle) Buddhism, a later form of the religion that spread through Tibet, China, Japan, Mongolia and Korea. At Wat Poman in Bangkok's Chinatown, Mahayana monks gather for prayer. Unlike Theravada monks, those in the Mahayana *sangha* only eat food prepared within their monasteries and do not take vows of celibacy.

PAUL CHESLEY

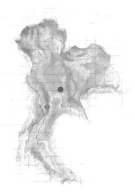

● **ABOVE:**

With big windows, room to stretch out and a ticket price of just 12 baht (50 cents) for an hour-long ride, third-class train cars are a comfortable alternative to Thai buses.

NICK KELSH

● **RIGHT:**

Near the Gulf of Thailand at Hua Hin, a truck carries migrant agricultural workers to the harvest. Pay in the sugar cane and pineapple fields averages 100 baht ($4) a day.

ROLAND NEVEU

Most Bangkok traffic police don surgical masks to protect themselves from the constant, toxic haze of automotive pollutants spewed by poorly maintained vehicles lacking pollution-control devices. The lead content of the city's air is three times the amount deemed safe in the United States. New environmental legislation mandating catalytic converters and government subsidized unleaded fuel may eventually help Bangkok residents breathe more easily.

BRUNO BARBEY

Workers put the finishing touches on new Volvos at the Thai-Swedish Assembly (TSA) plant, a joint venture between AB Volvo, Renault and the Swedish Motors Corporation of Thailand. Parts arriving from Sweden are assembled at the TSA plant outside Bangkok, which produces top-of-the-line Volvo sedans. TSA employees also enjoy top-of-the-line benefits, including free transportation to and from work, recreation facilities, free lunches, annual medical check-ups and the services of a full-time nurse.

SYLVIA PLACHY

Bangkok's "rush hour" lasts all day and night, letting up only briefly in the early morning hours. Part of the problem is a skyrocketing number of cars—500 new vehicles a day. Furthermore, Bangkok has far fewer streets than most Western cities. Only 8 percent of Bangkok is covered by roadways, compared with more than 20 percent of New York and London.

NICOLE BENGIVENO

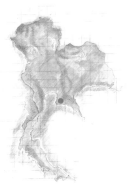

● **ABOVE AND RIGHT:**

Near Pattaya, a boisterous resort town on the Gulf of Thailand, neatly dressed orphans line up for a picture by *Day in the Life* photographer Mary Ellen Mark. The orphanage—founded by Father Brennan, a hearty Irish priest from Chicago—is funded in part by tourist donations. Later, Mark captured naptime at the orphanage.

MARY ELLEN MARK

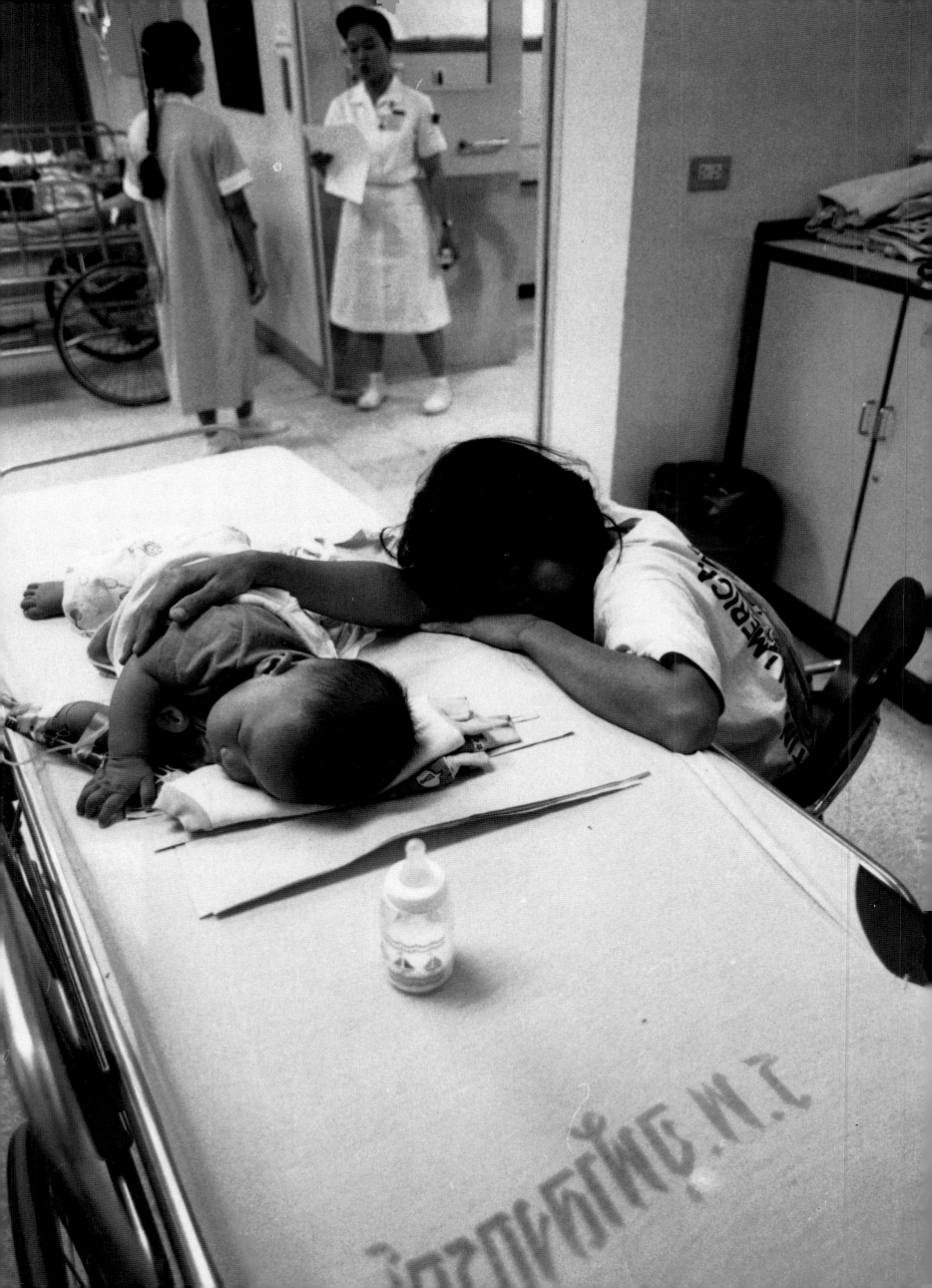

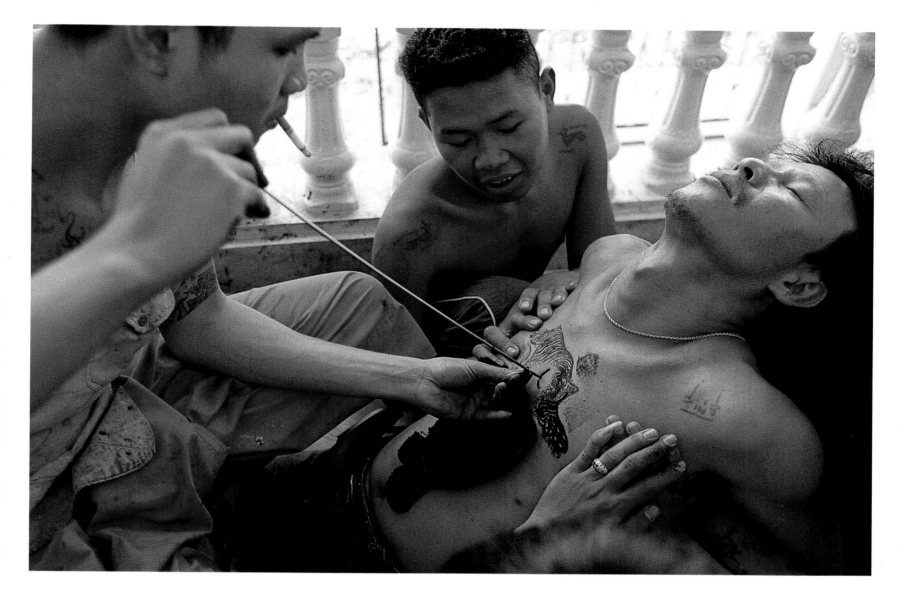

● **LEFT:**

Nuat boran, traditional Thai massage, is an ancient—and sometimes acrobatic—form of therapy that both relaxes and invigorates the patient. Widely available throughout Thailand, this healing art is taught by master practitioners at special monastery schools.

DANIEL LAINÉ

● **FAR LEFT:**

In the emergency room of Bangkok's Chulalongkorn Hospital, a mother surrenders to fatigue after waiting hours for a doctor to examine her baby for gastrointestinal problems.

SUSAN BIDDLE

● **ABOVE:**

Young men in Bangkok's Klong Toey slum area are tattooed with protective symbols, inscriptions and pictures of wild beasts. Using a steel needle, but no anesthetic, a monk at Wat Bang Phra punctures the skin of Noi Phothamin, creating the image of a tiger—a favorite design that symbolizes strength and speed.

SUSAN MEISELAS

● **PREVIOUS PAGES:**

In Sob Ruak—in the heart of the Golden Triangle—Thursday, February 24, was a mothers' day festival. Celebrants paraded to the temple compound, carrying offering trees festooned with money and gifts for the monks.

MICHAEL YAMASHITA

● **ABOVE:**

Apasara Hongsakul Chirathivat, Miss Universe of 1965 and a popular face in Thai high society, posed for photographer Douglas Kirkland—well-known for his portraits of glamorous Hollywood celebrities ranging from Marilyn Monroe to Jack Nicholson.

DOUGLAS KIRKLAND

● ABOVE:

Business leaders—including Dr. Chokchai Aksaranan, Chairman of the Federation of Thai Industries—celebrate at a cocktail party at a Bangkok hotel.

DOUGLAS KIRKLAND

● FOLLOWING PAGES:

A fisherman at sunset on the Mekong River near Chiang Khong. The broad waters of the Mekong divide Thailand and Laos, flowing 2,600 miles (4,180 kilometers) from the Tibetan plateau to the South China Sea.

MICHAEL YAMASHITA

Buddhist monks are bathed in the mystical light streaming into a cave near Khorat. Throughout the country, caves are imbued with spiritual significance. Many contain Buddha images and serve as meditation cells and assembly halls for monks. **DILIP MEHTA**

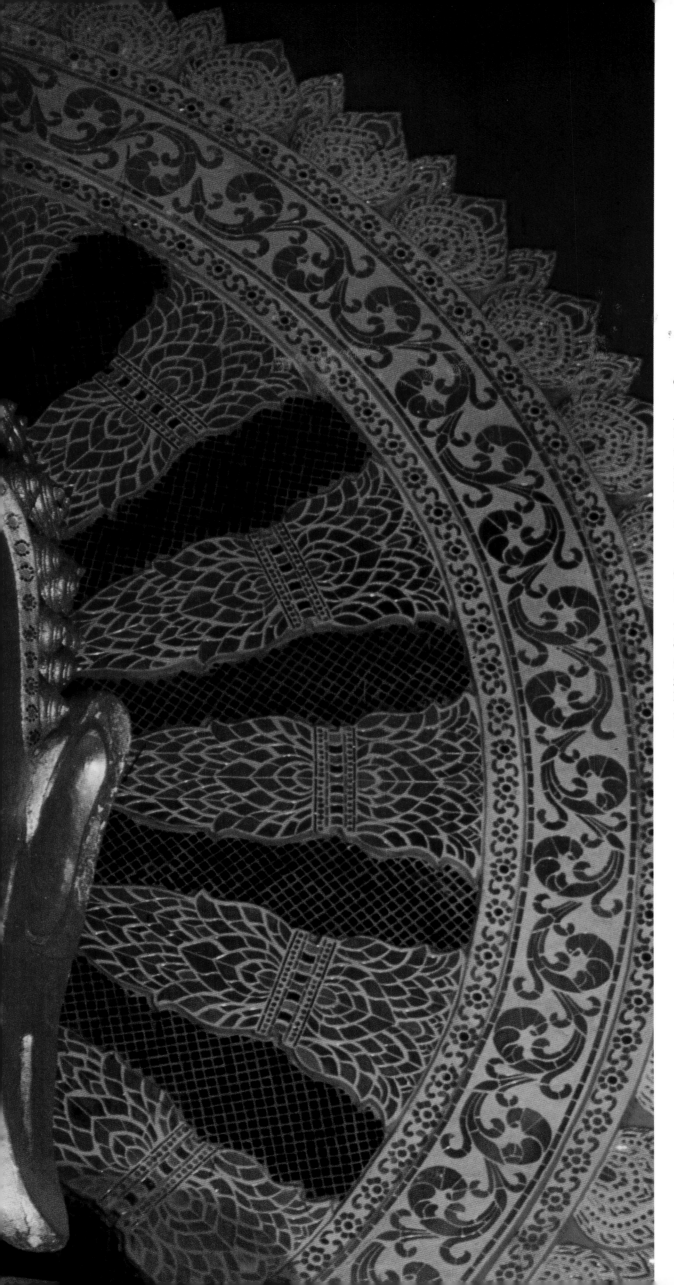

● **LEFT:**

Agolden Buddha image gazes down at worshipers at Wat Phra Sing, the 14th century Temple of the Lion Buddha in Chiang Mai. The pierced earlobes are a reminder of the Buddha's early life of princely luxury before he sought enlightenment.

LINDSAY HEBBERD

● **FOLLOWING PAGES:**

On the final day of the Chinese New Year celebration, worshipers jam the small Sanjao Pho Suea Buddhist temple in Bangkok's crowded Chinatown. By honoring the gods with candles and incense, they hope to gain health and prosperity in the coming year.

PAUL CHESLEY

Friendship flowers in the dusty Akha village of Gui Satai.

BARRY LEWIS

Children scatter corn for swarming pigeons at Sanam Luang, an elliptical field near the Grand Palace in Bangkok. Still venerated as the royal cremation ground, Sanam Luang draws picnickers, kite flyers, food vendors and all manner of Bangkok citizenry seeking refuge from the urban crush.

PORNVILAI CARR

At Mae Sot, a well-developed western outpost three miles (five kilometers) from the Myanmar border, a Burmese boy looks after cows owned by local Thai farmers. These bony Lampang whites and reds are kept primarily as dairy cattle. Mae Sot, which has a "Wild West" reputation, is not only a cattle trading center, but also a hub for frontier traffic in teak, gems and contraband. Its diverse population is made up of Thais, Burmese, Chinese and hill tribe peoples.

JAN BANNING

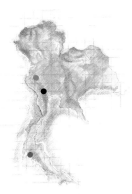

● **LEFT:**
The village mosque and stilt-legged houses of Koh Pannyi stand in the shadow of a limestone mountain in Phangnga Bay.
JOHN EVERINGHAM

● **PREVIOUS PAGES:**
Mist rises over the Khao Laem Reservoir at Sangklaburi. Formed by the damming of the Khwae Noi River in 1983, the sprawling reservoir covered trees and an entire town. The old town *chedis* become visible when the water level falls.
SHRIMP

● **FOLLOWING PAGES:**
Wat Tham Kao Noi, a Chinese Buddhist temple in Thai Muang, overlooks the peaceful Khwae Noi River in Kanchanaburi province. The two tallest spires represent the two strains of Buddhism in Thailand—a Theravada *chedi* on the left and a Chinese-style Mahayana pagoda on the right.
FRANK FOURNIER

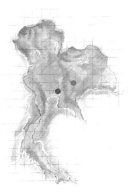

● **RIGHT:**
The sun sets beyond the gleaming office towers of Bangkok's Silom Road—one of the booming capital's main business centers.

SCOTT THODE

● **FOLLOWING PAGES:**
Facing the setting sun, Phra Sompong Umbuar meditates with three young novices in a quiet clearing at the Wat Wachiralongkorn monastery in Khorat.

DILIP MEHTA

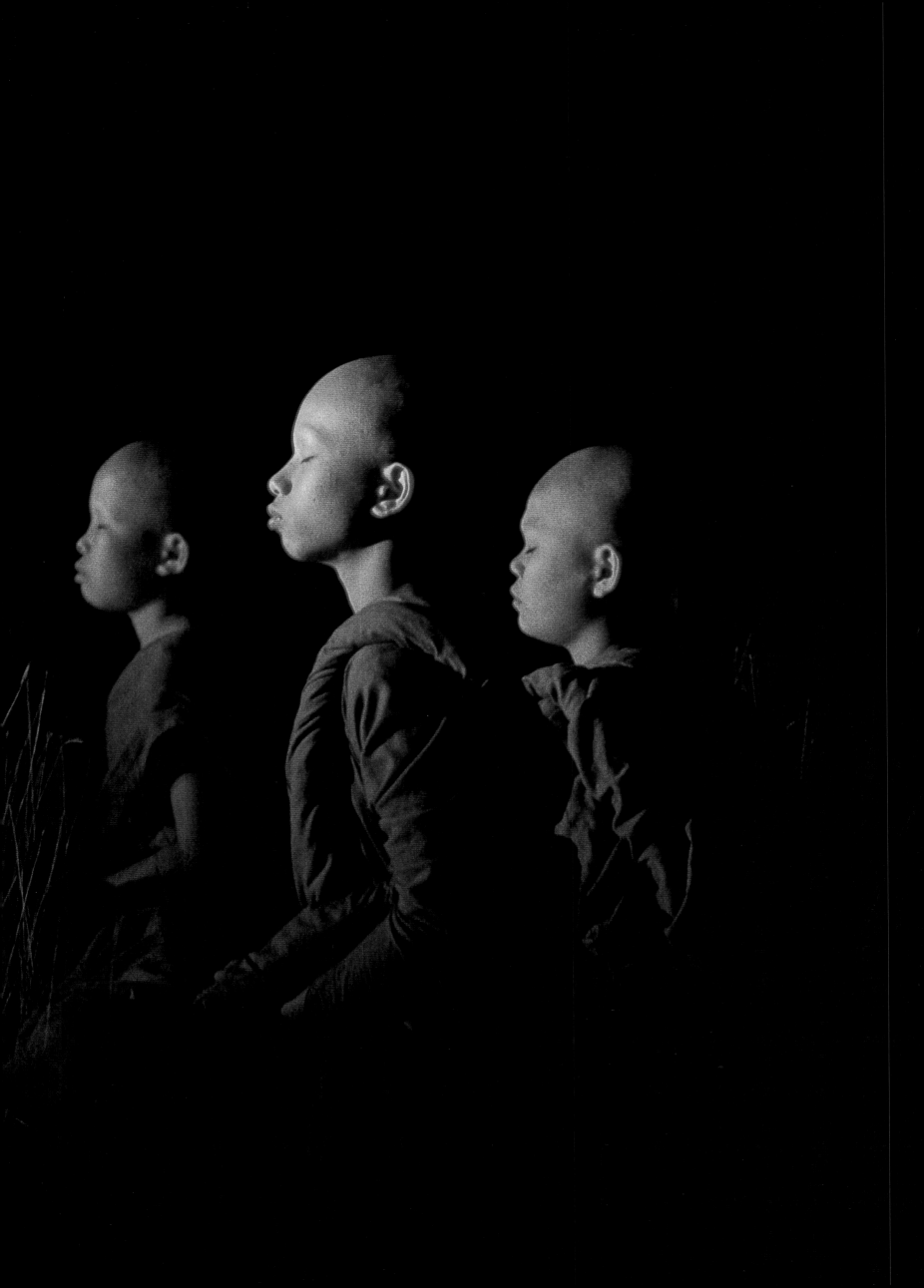

In the Gulf of Thailand, off Cha-am, trawlers set sail for a night of fishing. The fishermen use bright lights strung above their decks to lure schools of garupa, tuna, mackerel and snapper. Thailand's modern fishing fleet hauls in more than 2.5 million tons of fish a year. This harvest makes the kingdom one of the world's top ten seafood exporters, but raises concerns about overfishing in the Gulf of Thailand.

JAMES MARSHALL

A hilltop Buddha image, adorned with seven serpent heads, watches over the countryside below Wat Wachiralongkorn.

DILIP MEHTA

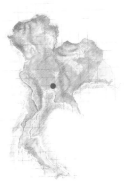

● RIGHT:

Between rounds at Ratchadamnoern Stadium in Bangkok, Wanghin Chaiwat, a *muay Thai* fighter, receives guidance from his manager, Ping Putorn. Thai boxers have a sacred relationship with their mentors, demonstrated in the five-minute *ram muay* dance of respect that boxers perform before each match.

First mentioned in 15th century accounts, muay Thai is a fierce martial art that was once a regular part of Thai military training. Until the 1920s, when regulations banned the practice, fighters routinely bound their hands with hemp or horsehide studded with ground glass. Fighters now wear lightly padded gloves, but the fiercest blows are delivered with barefoot kicks and punishing thrusts from knees and elbows. Despite the exhortations of his trainer, Chaiwat lost his match to champion Chamungpetch Chorchamung.

MAGGIE STEBER

● BELOW:

In Bangkok, night golfers hone their strokes at a driving range on Sukhumvit Road. Golf is one of Thailand's newest—and most lucrative—passions. Since 1989, the number of golf courses in the country has risen from 14 to more than 140. Golf club memberships, which cost up to $72,000 (1,800,000 baht)—are traded actively on a speculative market in Bangkok. Many of the most avid golfers in Thailand are Japanese tourists, who find it cheaper to fly to Thailand than to tee off in their own country, where club memberships can cost $500,000 to $1 million (12,500,000 to 25,000,000 baht).

SCOTT THODE

● **LEFT:**

Careening wildly through traffic, *tuk-tuks* are a cheap—if precarious—form of transportation through Bangkok's gridlocked streets.

DOUGLAS KIRKLAND

● **ABOVE:**

A three-block neon-lit strip called Patpong Road comes alive at sunset. With its dozens of bars and hundreds of shopping stalls, Patpong doubles as the center of Bangkok's prodigious sex industry and a huge outdoor mall.

RICK BROWNE

● **RIGHT:**

Office building construction
continues through the night
at Liberty Square in Bangkok's
financial district. Thailand's hard-
charging construction firms work
around-the-clock to finish projects
in record time.

SCOTT THODE

● **ABOVE:**

I n the library car of the luxurious
Eastern & Oriental Express, a palm
reader divines the future of Janet
Lubic, an American tourist from
Pittsburgh. According to the fortune-
teller, Lubic has "a good husband and
a bad relationship with a business
partner." Ms. Lubic, in fact, had just
broken up with a business associate
and was enjoying the train journey
from Bangkok to Singapore as a gift
from her husband.

RICK BROWNE

● **ABOVE:**

Actors prepare for an evening performance at the Thai Cultural Center in Bangkok.

ALEX WEBB

● **FOLLOWING PAGES :**

Workers in Bangkok tuck supplements inside the next day's edition of *Thai Rath*, Thailand's largest-circulation daily newspaper.

ABBAS

● **LEFT:**

S treet stalls continue to do a brisk business after nightfall in Phetchaburi town.

JAMES MARSHALL

● **ABOVE:**

S hoppers inspect imported apples and locally grown watermelon, mangoes, pineapples, coconuts and bananas at the Talad Kaset night market in Phuket.

PASCAL MAITRE

● **ABOVE:**

On shoot day, photographer Nevada Wier was in the tribal settlement of Pha Daeng, in mountainous northwestern Thailand. There, the Lahu Nyi (Red Lahu) celebrated the end of their eight-day New Year's festival. The granddaughter of the village headman, Khun Lawa, kept her hands warm against the cool night air, while young men and women courted, children played with balls and tops, and villagers danced around a spirit house until sunrise.

NEVADA WIER

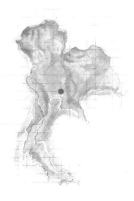

● **LEFT:**

A t the Chalermkrung Royal Theater in Bangkok, dancers perform the highly stylized movements of *khon*, the classical dance-drama of Thailand. Originally derived from the temple dances of India, khon arrived in Thailand via the courts of Angkor Wat, conquered by the Thais in the 16th century. Actors in ornate costumes employ graceful hand movements to recount the Ramakhien—the Thai version of the Indian epic, the Ramayana.

RICK RICKMAN

● **RIGHT:**
At Surat Thani's Hai-Lum Chinese temple, projectionists beam a horror film onto an outdoor canvas screen. Movies are also sometimes shown by traveling salesmen to attract customers.
ANTONIN KRATOCHVIL

● **PREVIOUS PAGES:**
Despite the elaborate costumes and severely painted faces, Chinese opera is an informal entertainment for families at provincial temple fairs and funerals. Traveling troupes, like these actors in Surat Thani on the southern peninsula, set up their own stage and scenery and perform late into the night, while audience members eat, nap and sometimes climb onto the stage.
ANTONIN KRATOCHVIL

Buddhist devotees in Kanchanaburi, carrying candles and incense sticks, circumambulate the *viharn* (assembly hall) three times on Magha Puja. In Buddhist tradition, the viharn is revered as a ship that carries the faithful to salvation, while candles represent a river of light. *Day in the Life* photographer Frank Fournier brings this concept to life photographically with an eight-second time exposure.

FRANK FOURNIER

● *A Day in the Life of Thailand* photographers and staff outside the Imperial Queen's Park Hotel in Bangkok. **JAMES MARSHALL**

EDITOR & PROJECT DIRECTOR
David Cohen

PROJECT CO-DIRECTORS
James Marshall
Rick Browne

DIRECTOR OF PHOTOGRAPHY
Peter Howe

DESIGNER
Tom Morgan, *Blue Design*

WRITERS
Susan Wels
Steve Van Beek

FINANCE DIRECTOR
Devyani Kamdar

PRODUCTION COORDINATOR
Barry Sundermeier

LOGISTICS COORDINATOR
Linda Lamb

PUBLICITY
Molly Schaeffer

PICTURE EDITORS
Howard Chapnick
Sandra Eisert, *The San Francisco Examiner*
Bert Fox, *The Philadelphia Inquirer*
Laurie Kratochvil
George Wedding

ASSIGNMENT EDITOR
Susy Barry
InnerAsia Expeditions, Hanoi

ASSIGNMENT COORDINATORS
Pornthip ("Addie") Samerton
Paiboon ("Pat") Sonjai
Tour East, Thailand

LOCATION CONSULTANTS
Jim Sano
Sarah Timewell
InnerAsia Expeditions, San Francisco

**INTERNATIONAL TRAVEL
COORDINATORS**
Kate Doty
Scott Montgomery
InnerAsia Expeditions, San Francisco

Sara Capes
Tour East, Viet Nam

COPY EDITOR
Amy Wheeler

STAFF PHYSICIAN
Robert ("Dr. Bob") Rabkin, M.D.

ATTORNEY
Philip Feldman
Coblentz, Cahen, McCabe & Breyer

GUIDES
Adisorn Sangsawadi
Amphol Udomkid
Aroon Buphachartnaichit
Bang-on Thokaew
Chana Ondej
Chawalit Likitratcharoen
Cherngchai Sutabutara
Duangrat Gituvirhakul
Jamnong Rungaree
Kasemcharti Chotichawong
Koravit Buddee
Naowarat Taebanpagul
Nirandorn Mekbot
Nopparat Janthata
Patravut Indrapatit
Pornchai Khummee
Pramuk Tekginda
Samran Hima
Samroeng Bunyawiwat
Sant Mekwai
Sattha Sornvijit
Seksan Sutthana
Somboon Thitatharn
Sompong Paywong
Supot Srisombat
Suriya Sasanakul
Suriyayut Wongchaiya
Suthep Chaimala
Vitthaya Phanphinich
Wanee Nuamthaisong
Watcharee Chattong
Yajit Kongkaew
Yaovamal Visanvit

STUDENT GUIDES
Annop Kunthathum
Apiradee Sukha-Akom
Boonya Mongkolsilpa
Kanit Vongchindarak
Kaniya Koh-Anatakul
Glenn LaSalle
Narathip Supunavong
Nongnoot Pichetkul
Phenrung Chiewcharnvalijkit
Pitsuda Chancharoen
Puneet Bajaj
Sanya Charuwan
Sarawuj Khonsungneun
Siriwan Tiralerd
Supaporn Sakolkittiwat
Thadithong Bhrammanee
Waraporn Subhschaturas
Weera Sirikijpanijkul

DRIVERS
Boonsong Sutthana
Chaliew Pengyot
Dang Chaithep
Jeerasak Bun U-Bon
Jongluk Jampasiri
Kittipong Nanthawanich
Nakorn Chumsiri
Niwat Kwanwang
Niyom Pattananwon
Pachern Nakarintorn
Paitoon Luangtao
Paitoon Muangnai
Pansak Viriyasiri
Patprayoon Isarasak Na Ayuthaya
Khun Pinit
Prateep Pho-In
Saipin Ondej
Sakda Somwong
Sombat Eiampoo
Somchart Niyasom
Khun Somsak
Song Prempeun
Surasak Wongthanee
Thongchai Sa-Ing Thong

PHOTOGRAPHERS' BIOGRAPHIES

ABBAS
Iranian/Paris
An Iranian transplanted to the West, Abbas has covered major political and social events for the past 23 years, primarily in the southern hemisphere. He has just completed a seven-year project on Islam around the world. Abbas is a member of Magnum, Paris.

JANE EVELYN ATWOOD
American/Paris
Jane Evelyn Atwood was born in New York in 1947 and has been living in France since 1971. A member of Contact Press Images since 1988, she works primarily in the tradition of documentary photography, following individuals or groups of people (usually on society's fringes) for long periods. She is the author of three books—two about French prostitutes in Paris and one about the French Foreign Legion. She has won various international prizes and was the first recipient of the W. Eugene Smith Award in 1980 for her work on the blind. In 1987, she won a World Press Prize for "Jean-Louis—Living and Dying with AIDS." In 1990, she received the *Paris Match* Grand Prix du Photojournalisme, and in 1991 received the Canon Photo Essay Award for her work in Soviet women's prisons. Her first retrospective, "Documents," was part of the Mois de la Photo in Paris in 1990-91.

JAN BANNING
Dutch/Nijmegen, Holland
Banning studied history before turning to freelance photography. He is published in many newspapers and magazines. His area of interest includes social, economic and political subjects in Asia, Europe, Africa and the US. Between 1988 and 1992, he made five trips to Vietnam, spending nearly six months in the country, with a grant from the Dutch Foundation for Art, Design and Architecture. The resulting book, *Vietnam:Doi Moi* , was published in 1993 by Focus of Amsterdam.

BRUNO BARBEY
French/Paris
Bruno Barbey was born in Morocco, and began his professional photography career in 1960 with the Swiss publisher Editions Rencontres which commissioned him to document several countries. Since joining Magnum Photos in 1966, he has covered stories on all continents, particularly in the Arab world. His photographic essays on such diverse locations as Sri Lanka, Nigeria and Morocco, among others, have been published in *The London Sunday Times, Esquire, Stern, Time, Life,* and *Paris Match*.

Barbey's photographs have been shown in numerous exhibitions, including the Bibliotheque Nationale in Paris, the Kunstmuseum in Zurich, The Photographers Gallery in London, the Olympus Gallery in Paris and most recently in the group exhibition "Magnum Concert" held at the Musee d'Art et Histoire in Fribourg, Switzerland. Institutions such as the Bibliotheque Nationale, the Musee Reattu in Arles and the International Center of Photography in New York contain Barbey's photographs in their permanent collections.

Publications featuring photographs by Barbey include *Naples* (1964), *Portugal* (1966), *Koweit* (1967), and *Ecose* (1968), all published by Editions Rencontre. Other books are *Ceylan: Sri Lanka* (1974), *Iran: Rebirth of a Timeless Empire* (1976), *Nigeria* (1978), *Bombay* (1979), *Poland* (1982) and *Le Bagon* (1984).

● A Buddha image in Bangkok's Chinatown. **STEVE MCCURRY**

NICOLE BENGIVENO
American/New York City
Bengiveno joined the staff of the *New York Daily News* in 1986 after eight years with the *San Francisco Examiner*. She has won numerous awards and has traveled throughout the world on assignments including Soviet Central Asia and Kazakhstan in 1989, Albania in 1991 for *National Geographic*, and most recently to mainland China and Cuba in 1993 for the *New York Daily News*. This is her twelfth *Day in the Life* book project.

SUSAN BIDDLE
American/Alexandria, Virginia
Susan Biddle is currently freelancing, having worked as a White House photographer during the Bush administration and the last year of the Reagan administration. Previously she worked at the *Denver Post* and *Topeka Capital Journal.*. She started her career at the Peace Corps, where she became Director of Photography. Susan has participated in several book projects, including *A Day in the Life of America, Baseball in America* and *Hong Kong: Here Be Dragons*.

RICK BROWNE
American/Scotts Valley, California
Co-director of *A Day in the Life of Thailand*, Browne is a photojournalist specializing in travel photography and environmental portraiture for both editorial and corporate clients. He recently received the silver medal from the Society of American Travel Writers. Browne was also director and co-editor of the book *Hong Kong: Here Be Dragons*, and is under contract as photographic consultant to the world-renowned Monterey Bay Aquarium. Browne is known as the world's greatest optimist and a very good cook.

PORNVILAI CARR
Thai/Bangkok
Khun Pornvilai started her career in photography in 1985 with Agence France Press. She moved to the Bangkok bureau of the Associated Press in 1991. She was injured in clashes between police and pro-democracy demonstrators on the streets of the Thai capital in 1992. Pornvilai, known widely by her nickname "Daeng," currently freelances out of Bangkok.

PETER CHARLESWORTH

British / Bangkok

Peter Charlesworth is based in Bangkok. His pictures appear in *Time, Newsweek, The New York Times Magazine* and various European publications. He is represented by the photographic agency SABA Press Photos.

PAUL CHESLEY

American / Aspen, Colorado

Chesley is a freelance photographer who has worked with *National Geographic* since 1975, traveling regularly to Europe and Asia. He has completed more than 35 projects for the Society. Solo exhibitions of his work have appeared in museums in London, Tokyo and New York. *A Day in the Life of Thailand* is the twelfth *Day in the Life* project for Chesley, a frequent contributor to *Life, Fortune, Time, Newsweek, Audubon, GEO* and *Stern*. Recent books including his work are *The Circle of Life, Mauritius, Hawaii, Colorado* and *America: Then & Now*. Paul shoots more film than any other *Day in the Life* photographer.

JOHN EVERINGHAM

Australian / Bangkok

Born in Australia in 1949, John dropped out of high school and left home at 16 years old to travel from Australia to London—by motorcycle.

His 300cc bike brought him to Vietnam in early 1968 during the Tet offensive on Saigon. Soon he became friends with the photojournalism crowd, and began taking photos to sell to the wire services and visiting journalists. By the end of the war in 1975, he was in Laos working as reporter for the BBC, *The Far Eastern Economic Review* and *Newsweek*.

The only western journalist in Indochina after the war, Everingham was thrown into jail as a CIA spy by the Lao communists in 1977. In 1978, he moved to Bangkok, where he turned increasingly to magazine work and photography. Everingham has been based in Bangkok ever since. His publishing company ARTASIA produces some of the highest quality periodicals in Thailand, including *PHUKET Magazine, Fah Tahi*, and *Heritage Magazine*.

John rescued, then married, his Laotian girlfriend from the communist days, Keo, and they have two sons, aged 12 and 8.

He is the Black Star correspondent in Thailand. Magazines in which he has been published include: *Newsweek, Time, The Smithsonian, National Geographic, International Wildlife, GEO , Harpers, Stern*, and countless airline magazines.

NEIL FARRIN

British / Hong Kong

Neil Farrin arrived in Hong Kong in 1977 after five years as a photojournalist for the British press, including *The Times of London* and *The Telegraph*. He has traveled on assignment in such diverse areas as Scotland, the United States, Germany, Sweden, Australia, New Zealand and Southeast Asia . His photography includes corporate and advertising work. Farrin's journalistic work has appeared in *GEO, Time, Newsweek, The Sunday Times* and the book *Hong Kong: Here Be Dragons*. Farrin currently runs Profile Photo Library in Hong Kong and Singapore.

FRANK FOURNIER

French / New York City

Fournier's work has appeared in a broad array of magazines and journals including *Time, Life, Paris-Match*, and *The New York Times Magazine*. He won the 1986 World Press Photo Premier Award, and recently he has focused on women's rights in Sarajevo and juvenile violence in Alaska.

PATRICK GAUVAIN (SHRIMP)

British / Bangkok

Shrimp was conceived in Kensington Church Street, London on rather a cold night and born in Penang, Malaysia on rather a hot morning just after the end of the Second World War in the middle of the 20th century.

After traveling the globe as a child, he received an education in British public schools peppered with canings and homosexuality. "Shrimp," incidentally, is a gross nickname from public school. It refers to his diminutive height, but belies his many talents. (He may be small, but he is perfectly formed.)

Shrimp's first job was at Battersea Fun Fair as an assistant to the Spider Lady. He was spotted there by a horrified school friend who immediately got him a position in an advertising agency. Playing in the

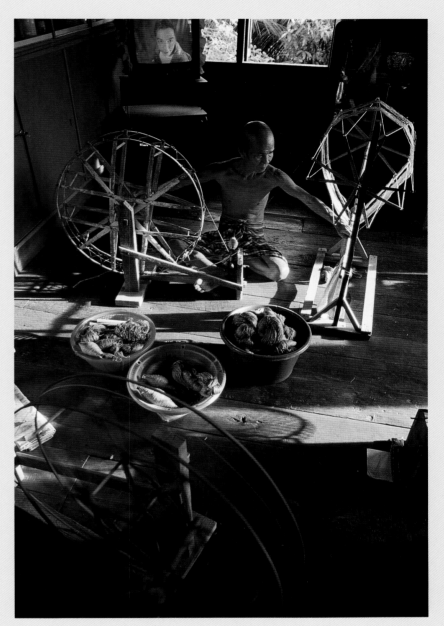

● A silk spinner in Thongchai. **MARK GREENBERG**

agency's darkroom led to the discovery of various chemicals—legal and illegal.

With this basic training, Shrimp was ready to pull back the black curtains and venture into the world with a Brownie 127 Automatic. Success was instantaneous, and soon Shrimp was cavorting in the creative corridors of Conde Nast, Young & Rubicam, McCann Erickson, *Playboy* and *Penthouse*.

Soon fame took Shrimp to the Far East (in a third class cabin) on the Trans-Siberian Express via Nahodka to Japan. There he began a new career as a pimp in the Ginza. Armed with a Nikon F, he catalogued the late '60s in Shinjuku. After a short stint at Japan's hottest pinup magazine *Heibon Punch, Asahi Shimbun* spotted Shrimp's extraordinary talents and sent him

to Vietnam. Arriving in the middle of the 1968 Tet Offensive was bad planning. Shrimp immediately fled to Angkor Wat where the aesthetics of Asian culture stirred his loins—as did the tea dancers in Siem Riep. Shrimp's three month stay was rudely interrupted by the Khmer Rouge, and he fled to the Thai border arriving just in time for a village temple fair.

After a few euphoric years in the floating brothels of Klong Saen Sap and the opium dens of forbidden Bangkok, Shrimp joined Associated Communications Corporation, a Thai advertising agency, as their photographer/art director. During this time, he also worked on several feature film productions including *The Man with the Golden Gun* and *The Deer Hunter*.

PHOTOGRAPHERS' BIOGRAPHIES

Shrimp Studios was founded in 1976, producing a range of "Shrimp Products" including calendars, books, watches and cards of exotic Asian ladies while handling advertising clients such as The Peninsula Group, Shangrila Hotel, KLM Royal Dutch Airlines, Volvo, Jim Thompson and Thai Silk. In 1989, the agency side of the business merged with BSB Worldwide. In 1991, Shrimp resigned from BSB and rebuilt Shrimp Studios as a small creative advertising agency specializing in the travel trade. Shrimp has contributed to the book, *Seven Days in the Kingdom*, produced his own book, *Thai Girls* and has photographed many articles for Hong Kong and European glamour magazines. He recently completed a book commemorating the tenth anniversary of the Hilton International Bangkok titled *Nai Lert Park*. He has one beautiful son of two and a half years whom he loves very much.

MARK GREENBERG
American/New York City
Mark is a founding partner of the feature photo agency Visions based in New York City. His photographs have won awards in the World Press Photo Competition and have been displayed in galleries and museums throughout the world. He has been working on a long-term project in Venezuela with the Yanomami Indians and is deeply involved with a humanitarian organization committed to saving this culture from extinction.

LORI GRINKER
American/New York City
Lori Grinker began her career in 1980, while still a student at Parsons School of Design, when an assignment about a young boxer was published as a cover story by *Inside Sports*. At that time, she met 14-year-old Mike Tyson, whom she has continued to photograph through the years. Her work has taken her to the Middle East, Southeast Asia, Eastern Europe, the Soviet Union, Africa and throughout the United States. She has been traveling extensively in Cambodia and Vietnam since February 1989. Her photographs have been exhibited in museums and galleries in Paris, Amsterdam, Arles and New York and have been featured in *Life*, *The New York Times*

Magazine, *Newsweek*, *People*, *The Sunday Times Magazine* (London), *Stern*, *GEO* and *Il Venerdi*.

Grinker has been a member of Contact Press Images since 1988. Her book, *The Invisible Thread: A Portrait of Jewish American Women* (1989), explores the diverse experience of Jewish women in the United States. A collection of images from the book toured the United States from 1990 to 1992. She is currently at work on two new book projects, one dealing with indigenous peoples and their sacred relationship to the environment and one on the effects of war on veterans around the world.

CAROL GUZY
American/Washington, D.C.
Carol Guzy was born and raised in Bethlehem, Pennsylvania where she completed her studies at Northampton County Area Community College, graduating with an Associate's degree in Registered Nursing. A change of heart led her to the Art Institute of Fort Lauderdale in Florida to study photography. She graduated in 1980 with an Associate degree. While at the Art Institute, she interned at the *Miami Herald*, and upon graduation was hired as a staff photographer. She spent eight years there before moving to Washington, DC in 1988 to work for *The Washington Post*, where she is currently employed. Her assignments include both domestic and foreign stories. She is a member of the National Press Photographers Association and the White House News Photographers Association. She has been honored with numerous awards, including the prestigious Pulitzer Prize in Spot News photography. She was twice named Photographer of the Year by the National Press Photographers Association.

STEVE HART
American/New York City
Steve Hart was born in Texas in 1962. In 1986, moved to New York and began work as a freelance photographer. He has been the recipient of The Gordon Parks Award, The New York Foundation for the Arts Award, and The Leica Medal of Excellence. He is currently working on a project documenting a family in the Bronx where both parents have AIDS.

DAVID ALAN HARVEY
American/Washington, D.C.
David has photographed 25 articles for *National Geographic* with subjects ranging from Vietnam to American Indian ceremonies. His work has also appeared in *The New York Times Sunday Magazine*, *Life* and *Sports Illustrated*. Harvey is currently a nominee for membership in Magnum. He is a former National Press Photographers; Association Magazine Photographer of the Year. Harvey has worked on five previous *Day in the Life* projects.

LINDSAY HEBBERD
American/Irving, Texas
Hebberd is a free-lance photographer who travels extensively, documenting cultures and traditions around the world. Represented by Woodfin Camp & Associates, her work appears in numerous cultural, educational and travel publications. In 1991-92, Hebberd's solo exhibit, *Cultural Portraits of Indonesia*, toured America. A complementary book and an international tour are planned. Currently she is producing another exhibition, *Cultural Portraits of India*.

ROBERT HOLMES
British/Mill Valley, California
Robert Holmes is one of the world's foremost travel photographers. He was the first person to receive the Society of American Travel Writers' Travel Photographer of the Year award twice, in 1990 and 1992. His work regularly appears in major travel publications, including *National Geographic*, *GEO*, *Travel & Leisure* and *Islands*. He has 15 books in print. His photographs have been exhibited widely and are included in both corporate and museum collections.

CATHERINE KARNOW
American/San Francisco
Born in Hong Kong and based in San Francisco, Karnow is known for both her vivid portraits and travel photography. She has worked extensively in France, Scotland, Hong Kong, Los Angles and Vietnam. Among her books are *Adventures on the Scotch Whisky Trail* and the *Insight Guides* to France, Provence, Los Angeles, and Washington, D.C. Represented by Woodfin Camp,

Karnow also contributes frequently to *Smithsonian*, *Islands* and *Figaro*. She participated in *A Day in the Life of Hollywood*.

ED KASHI
American/San Francisco
Ed Kashi is a freelance photojournalist based in San Francisco whose work has appeared in *National Geographic*, *Time*, *Fortune*, *GEO*, *Life*, *Smithsonian*, *London Independent Magazine*, *Newsweek*, *Forbes* and *The New York Times Magazine*, among many other publications. He has spent the past three years with *National Geographic*, shooting cover stories on the Kurds, water problems in the Middle East and the Crimea. The story about the Kurds, which Ed researched and proposed, took him to Iraq, Iran, Syria, Turkey, Lebanon and Germany for eight grueling months in refugee camps and bombed-out Kurdish villages. It will be published in book form by Pantheon in 1995.

Kashi won a 1991 National Endowment for the Arts grant for his three years of documentary work on the Loyalists in Northern Ireland, widely published in the United States, Britain, Spain, Sweden, Japan, Canada and Italy.

As a documentary photographer, Kashi spends much of the year on the road working on topics of concern or interest to him. He has dealt with the heroin problem in Poland, culture and nightlife in Berlin, the return of Soviet veterans from Afghanistan as well as life in Eastern Europe. His latest personal project took him to Cairo to explore the City of the Dead. This story will be published in *Audubon* and *The Observer Magazine* in London.

NICK KELSH
American/Philadelphia
A native of North Dakota, Kelsh has produced award-winning photos for *Time*, *Life*, *Newsweek*, *National Geographic*, *Forbes*, *Fortune*, and *Business Week*. In 1986, he left the *Philadelphia Inquirer* to co-found Kelsh Wilson Design, a company that specializes in design and photography for annual reports and other corporate publications. Kelsh pictures are featured on the covers of *A Day in the Life of China*, *America: Then & Now* and *The Jews in America*. Kelsh sends out great Christmas cards.

● An iron monger in Bangkok. **NICK KELSH**

HIROJI KUBOTA
Japanese / Tokyo

Born in 1939 in Tokyo, Kubota graduated with a Bachelor of Arts in Political Science from Waseda University, Tokyo, in 1962. He lived in New York and Chicago from 1962 until 1967 and became a freelance photographer in New York in 1965. Kubota has been a member of the renowned Magnum photo agency since 1971. His work has been published and exhibited worldwide, and has been included in many books. His many awards include the prestigious Mainichi Art Award.

DANIEL LAINÉ
French / Paris

Lainé started his career as a freelance photographer for *Liberation* and has worked for *Partir* and *Grand Reportages*, completing numerous travel stories in South America and Africa. Lainé has been a correspondent in Western and Central Africa for Agence France Presse and a staff photographer for *Actuel*. Lainé's pictures have been featured in *A Day in the Life of America*, *A Day in the Life of Spain* and *The Circle of Life*. His own books include *Indios*, *Black Faces* and *Kings of Africa*.

SARAH LEEN
American / Arlington, Virginia

Sarah Leen was born in Sparta, Wisconsin in 1952. As an Army brat, she lived in Canada, Europe and several locations in the U.S. before settling in the Midwest. In 1974, she received a B.A. in Fine Arts from the University of Missouri and continued there with graduate work in journalism. In 1979, she was recognized as College Photographer of the Year and interned at the *National Geographic* where she worked in New England on a book about America's mountains and in Uganda on a post-Idi Amin story.

Leen began her professional career in earnest with an internship at the *Arizona Daily Star* in Tucson. From there, she moved to the *Topeka (Kansas) Capitol Journal*, *The Columbia (Missouri) Daily Tribune* and *The Philadelphia Inquirer*. As a staff photographer for five years at the *Inquirer*, she covered news stories

ranging from Beiruit to South Africa. In 1986, she won an honorable mention in the Robert Kennedy Awards for her story about a couple coping with Alzheimer's disease. Leen has participated in the Missouri Photo Workshop as an instructor for four years.

Since leaving the *Inquirer*, Leen has joined Matrix International, a New York-based photo agency, and has worked for *National Geographic* in the U.S., Canada and Siberia. She has also been published in *Time*, *GEO*, *Audubon* and *The London Daily Telegraph Sunday Magazine*. Leen has participated in several *Day in the Life* books as well as *One Earth*, *The Power to Heal*, and a book documenting the 1993 presidential inauguration, titled *An American Reunion*.

BARRY LEWIS
British / London

Originally a chemistry teacher, Lewis holds a Master's degree from the Royal College of Art and is a founding member of Network Photographers. He shoots regularly for *Life*, *National Geographic*, and *The Sunday Times*, and has participated in many *Day in the Life* books. He was the 1991 recipient of World Press Photo's Oscar Barnack Award for his work in Romania.

PASCAL MAITRE
French / Paris

Maitre has photographed conflicts the world over and has published his work in *GEO*, *Stern*, *Time*, *Life* and *Le Figaro*. He has published three books: *Rwanda* (1991), *Barcelona* (1989) and *Zaire* (1985). In 1986, Maitre won a World Press Photo award for his work in Iran. He is associated with the agency GLMR Associés/SAGA Images.

MARY ELLEN MARK
American / New York City

Mary Ellen Mark has achieved worldwide visibility through numerous photo essays in magazines such as *Vogue*, *L'Uomo*, *GQ*, *Life*, *Rolling Stone*, *New York Times Magazine*, *Mirabella*, *Stern*, and the *London Sunday Times Magazine*. She is recognized as one of our most respected and

DOUGLAS KIRKLAND
Canadian / Los Angeles

Kirkland is one of the world's best-known glamour and personality photographers. His 30 years in the business include camera work with Marilyn Monroe, Judy Garland, Barbra Streisand and Christie Brinkley. He was a founding member of Contact Press Images, and his books include *Light Years* (1989) and *Icons* (1993). He has been married to the beautiful and vivacious Francoise Kirkland for more than 25 years.

ANTONIN KRATOCHVIL
Czechoslovakian / New York City

Born in Czechoslovakia in 1947, Kratochvil has been working in the U.S.

as a freelance photographer since 1972. He continues to travel the world on assignment for *Discover Magazine*, *Newsweek*, *The New York Times*, *The Los Angeles Times*, *Smithsonian* and *Condé Nast Traveler*. His work has appeared in numerous books, and he was named 1991 Photojournalist of the Year by the International Center of Photography. In 1992, he won a silver medal from the Art Directors Club of New York and was awarded the 1994 Leica Medal of Excellence. Although Kratochvil is the most politically incorrect person alive, he has a wonderful spirit. No problem, man.

influential photographers, and her images of our world's diverse cultures have become landmarks in the field of documentary photography. A photo essay on runaway children in Seattle became the basis of her academy-award-nominated film *Streetwise* (directed and photographed by her husband, Martin Bell) and a book by the same title.

Mark's photographs have been exhibited worldwide and a retrospective, Mary Ellen Mark: Twenty-five Years is currently on an international tour. Among her many awards are three fellowships from the National Endowment for the Arts, the Photographer of the Year Award from the Friends of Photography, the World Press Award for Outstanding Body of Work Throughout the Years, the Victor Hasselblad Cover Award, two Robert F. Kennedy Awards and the Creative Arts Award Citation for Photography at Brandeis University. She has published nine books including *The Photojournalist ; Two Women Explore the Modern World: Mark and Leibovitz* (1974), *Passport* (1974), *Ward 81* (Simon and Schuster, 1979), *Falkland Road* (1981), *Mother Teresa's Mission of Charity in Calcutta* (1985), *The Photo Essay: Photographers at work, Streetwise* (second printing, 1992) and *Mary Ellen Mark: Twenty-five Years* (1991).

Indian Circus (1993), is her most recently published book. Last year, she was the associate producer of the major motion picture, *American Heart*, directed by her husband, Martin Bell. Besides her book and magazine work Mark has photographed several advertising campaigns. She is represented by Art & Commerce.

JAMES MARSHALL
American/New York
James Marshall began photography in a basement darkroom at age 15, and first sold pictures made at the local car races shortly thereafter. Raised in Japan and Europe, he returned to the U.S. to study painting and sculpture, earning an MFA degree from Pratt Institute in New York City. After a brief teaching career he returned to his roots in photography and for the past 15 years has traveled extensively in Europe and Asia contributing work to international publications including *Newsweek, The New York Times, Travel & Leisure, Christian Science Monitor, Smithsonian,* and *U.S. News & World Report.* Co-founder of Pacific Rim Concepts, he produced and edited *Hong Kong: Here be Dragons,* published to critical praise in 1992. In 1987 he was project director of *Document: Brooklyn,* involving 45 photographers recording one week in the life of this mythic American community. For the past three years he has been documenting the life of a Sihk immigrant family in New York City. A former Outward Bound assistant instructor, Marshall is always in search of a good adventure. He is co-director of *A Day in the Life of Thailand,* and personally dedicates this book to his two children, Nathan and Heather.

STEVE McCURRY
American/New York City
Steve McCurry does not consider himself a war photographer, but in the past six years he has traveled throughout Asia, the Far and Middle East, taking pictures of international and civil conflict. He was smuggled into Afghanistan, has photographed along the Thai-Cambodian border, made his way through bombed-out Beirut and visited the front of the Iran-Iraqi war. The images he brings back create an empathy for the innocent civilians caught up in war.

In 1980 McCurry's coverage of the Afghanistan war published in *Time* won him the Overseas Press Club's Robert Capa Gold Medal. In 1984 he was named Magazine Photographer of the Year in the University of Missouri and Canon contest. That same year he won four first prizes in the World Press Photo Contest. Submission for each contest included, in part, three extensive photo essays produced for *National Geographic*: "Afghan Border," "Monsoons: Life Breath of Half the World," and "By Rail Across the Indian Subcontinent."

McCurry's material from the Indian railroad story was expanded into a book, *The Imperial Way: Making Tracks from Peshawar to Chittagong,* published in 1985, by Houghton-Mifflin.

McCurry began his career as a staff photographer on *Today's Post* newspaper near Philadelphia. After 18 months there, he left to freelance for magazines in India, Pakistan and Nepal. In 1979, before the Russians invaded, he crossed into Afghanistan with the Mujahideen, and was among the first to reveal the growing conflict there. McCurry recently completed a six-month assignment on the Philippines for *National Geographic*.

JOHN W. McDERMOTT
American/Bangkok
McDermott began his career 15 years ago in his native state of Arkansas where he worked in both the commercial advertising and magazine photojournalism fields. His editorial work has been published regularly in numerous regional and national publications. In 1988 he moved to Los Angeles where for three years he worked in the feature film industry. He is now based in Bangkok and is the Chief Photographer for *Manager Magazine,* for which he covers an extensive variety of subjects and stories in the Asia-Pacific region.

JOE MCNALLY
American/New York City
Joe McNally is a freelance photographer based near New York City. He began his career in 1976 as a copyboy at the *New York Daily News,* but spent most of the late seventies shooting for clients such as *The New York Times,* AP and UPI. For two years he worked as the network still photographer for ABC television, covering news and sports.

● Riding the rollercoaster at Dan Namarit amusement park outside Bangkok.
PASSAKORN PAVILAI

McNally left ABC in 1981 to freelance for magazines. He began working for *Life* magazine in 1984 where he is a contributing photographer. He was a contract photographer for *Sports Illustrated* for six years, and has shot cover stories for *National Geographic, Life, Time, Newsweek, Sports Illustrated, Fortune* and *New York Magazine.*

He has won several National Press Photographers' Association Picture of the Year contests, winning first place in magazine illustration in 1988, as well as a Page One Award from the Newspaper Guild of New York in 1986. McNally has taught at the Eddie Adams Workshop for six years and has lectured on the NPPA Flying Short Course and the *National Geographic* Masters of Contemporary Photography Series. He has worked on numerous *Day in the Life* projects and was a featured exhibitor at the 1991 Festival of Photojournalism in Perpignan, France.

Joe was described by *American Photo* as "perhaps the most versatile photojournalist working today" and listed in their 1993 edition of the 100 most important people in photography. He and his wife, Michele McNally, have two daughters, Caitlin and Claire.

DILIP MEHTA
Canadian/New Delhi
A founding member of Contact Press Images, Mehta began his career in 1971 as a graphic designer before turning to photography and documentary filmmaking. He has covered such diverse subjects as the Bhopal tragedy and political developments in India, Pakistan, the U.S. and Afghanistan. Mehta's pictorial essays have been published in *Time, Newsweek, GEO, Bunte, The New York Times, Paris Match, Figaro, The London Sunday Times,* and other major publications around the world. He has won two World Press Photo Gold Awards and the Overseas Press Club Award.

SUSAN MEISELAS
American/New York City
Susan Meiselas received her masters in education from Harvard University and her undergraduate degree from Sarah Lawrence College. She ran workshops for

teachers and children in New York's South Bronx, and supported by grants from the National Endowment for the Arts and the state arts commissions of South Carolina and Mississippi, she set up film and photography programs in rural southern schools.

Meiselas' first major photographic essay focused on the lives of carnival strippers in New England. She joined Magnum Photos in 1976.

Meiselas' coverage of hostilities in Central America has been published worldwide by *The New York Times Magazine, The London Sunday Times, Time, GEO, Paris Match* and *Machete* among others. She won the Robert Capa Gold Medal from the Overseas Press Club in 1979 for her work in Nicaragua. Her two books are *Carnival Strippers* (1976) and *Nicaragua* (1981). Meiselas was an editor and contributor to the book *El Salvador: The Work of Thirty Photographers* and editor of *Chile From Within.*

Recently, Meiselas has been researching and photographing *In the Shadow of History: Kurdistan* for Random House. She has co-directed two films: *Living at Risk: The Story of a Nicaraguan Family* (1986) and *Pictures From a Revolution* (1991). Meiselas has also received the Leica Award for Excellence and the Photojournalist of the Year Award from the American Society of Magazine Photographers. In 1992, Meiselas was named a MacArthur Fellow. She received a Photographer's Fellowship from the National Endowment of the Arts in 1984 and was awarded an honorary degree in Fine Arts from Parsons School of Design in 1986.

CLAUS C. MEYER
German/Rio de Janeiro
The winner of many prizes and awards, Meyer was selected in 1985 by *Communications World* as one of the top annual-report photographers in the world. His excellence in color photography has been recognized by Kodak and Nikon, and in 1981 he won a Nikon International Grand Prize. He has published several books on Brazil, most recently a book on the Amazon in 1993.

ROBIN MOYER
American/Manila
Time magazine photographer Robin Moyer is one of Asia's most versatile and experienced shooters. In 1992, he won the Press Photo of the Year Award in the World Press Photo competition and the Robert Capa Gold Medal Citation from the Overseas Press Club of America for his coverage of the war in Lebanon.

ROLAND NEVEU
French/Bangkok
Born in France in 1950, Roland Neveu was based in Bangkok from 1979-1983, covering all of Asia for the Gamma Agency of Paris and New York. From 1983-1986, he worked in New York for Gamma-Liaison and *Time* magazine. From 1986-1992, Neveu took on Hollywoodworking as a "Special" and movie set photographer for clients such as Columbia Pictures, Carolco, Universal Pictures and 20th Century Fox. He also worked for several move directors including Oliver Stone (4 films), Brian DePalma and Ridley Scott. His photos have been made into posters for *Thelma & Louise, Rambo III* and *Casualites of War* among others.

In 1992 Neveu returned to Bangkok where he set up a publishing company specializing in pocket guides on Asian destinations.

BRIAN PALMER
American/Washington, D.C.
Palmer is currently a staff photographer for *U.S. News & World Report.* Formerly a freelancer, his work has appeared in *Time, Newsweek, Liberation, The National Law Journal, The New York Times, New York Times Magazine, Ms.,* Associated Press, *The Village Voice, The Chronicle of Higher Education, L.A. Weekly* and the recent book, *The African Americans.*

PASSAKORN PAVILAI
Thai/Bangkok
Passakorn Pavilai has a wide range of photographic experience. He was a photographer for the Thai Junior Encyclopaedia Under Royal Patronage, a photographer in the Satit-Chulalongkorn Photographic Club, Director of Picture

Project Co., Ltd., and a photographer for *Fashion Magazine.* Khun Passakorn is president of Satit Chulalongkorn Photography Club, president of the Satit Chulalongkorn Photo Contest, committee member of the Photographic Education Club at Chulalongkorn University, and President of the 16th Nationwide Student Photo Contest in 1982.

KRAIPIT PHANVUT
Thai/Bangkok
Phanvut began his career as a freelance photographer for the *Bangkok Post* in 1972. He has been chief photographer for United Press International in Bangkok, affiliated with Agence France Press and is currently SIPA Press's representative in Asia and the Pacific. His photographs have been published in various leading magazines and newspapers worldwide, including *Time, Newsweek, Paris Match, Stern, Bunte, Figaro, Fortune, Forbes* and *New York Times.* He was a contributor to the books *A Salute to Singapore* and *Seven Days in the Kingdom.* Phanvut received an award in the World Press Photo Contest 1977 and was nominated for a Pulitzer prize in 1978.

SYLVIA PLACHY
American/New York City
Sylvia Plachy's photographs have appeared in many publications. Her own book, *Unguided Tour,* won the Infinity Award from the International Center of Photography in 1990. Her most recent exhibit, *The Call of the Street,* was shown at the Whitney Museum at Philip Morris in 1993. Her photographs are in the collection of the Museum of Modern Art and the Metropolitan Museum in New York. She is currently working on books about Eastern Europe and about "red light" districts in the United States.

LARRY PRICE
American/Fort Worth, Texas
A native Texan, Price began his photographic career at the *El Paso Times.* Later, he worked for the *Fort Worth Star-Telegram,* where he won a Pulitzer Prize for his coverage of the 1980 Liberian coup. His photographs from El Salvador and Angola for the *Philadelphia*

PHOTOGRAPHERS' BIOGRAPHIES

Inquirer won him a second Pulitzer in 1985. His work has been honored by the Overseas Press Club, the National Press Photographers Association, the Associated Press and the World Press competition. Price is a seasoned contributor to the *Day in the Life* series.

RICK RICKMAN

American/Laguna Nigel, California
Rick Rickman has been working as a photographer for 17 years, and has been assigned major stories all over the world. He contributes regularly to *Time* and *National Geographic* magazines. In 1985, he was presented the Pulitzer Prize for Spot News Photography. Some of his favorite assignments have been with past *Day in the Life* projects. He is a very happy guy who laughs a lot.

GALEN ROWELL

American/Albany, California
Galen Rowell, recognized as one of the world's foremost naturalist-photographers, specializes in the Earth's wild places. He has been on 24 trips to the Himalayas as well as to both poles. His work often appears in *National Geographic, Life, Outdoor Photography, Audubon* and Sierra Club calendars as well as in his own eleven books, most recently *Galen Rowell's Vision: The Art of Adventure Photography.*

STEVE RUBIN

American/Baltimore, Maryland
Rubin's work is influenced by the documentary tradition of the 1930s and by his academic training in sociology. Undergraduate fieldwork among Gypsies led him to documentary photography, and since then, he has photographed the plight of Kurdish refugees, the destruction of the Ecuadorian rain forest, political turmoil in Pakistan and the transition to democracy in Chile. Closer to home, he has covered stories that include illegal immigration, the health care crisis and the not-so-romantic life of hoboes. He is currently an Alicia Patterson Foundation Fellow, completing a long-term photo essay, "Poverty in Vacationland: Life in a Backwoods Maine Community." He has been honored with the Leica Medal of Excellence, a New York Foundation for

● Kite flying near the Grand Palace in Bangkok. **JAMES MARSHALL**

the Arts Photography Fellowship, and an Award of Excellence from the National Press Photographers competition. He was a finalist for the W. Eugene Smith Award in Humanistic Photography in 1992 and 1993. His work has been published in *The New York Times Magazine, The Independent Magazine, Stern, GEO, L'Express, Time, Newsweek, The Village Voice* and *Outtakes* among others. He is represented by JB Pictures, New York.

JEFFERY ALLAN SALTER

American/Miami, Florida
In high school, all his classmates called him "the cameraman." Now they know him as Jeffery Allan Salter, the award-

winning photojournalist who has covered such global events as the bombing of the Pan Am airliner over Lockerbie, Scotland, and the deadly Haitian elections of November 1987. Currently, Salter is a staff photographer with *The Miami Herald.* Previously, he worked for *Newsday, The Bergen Record, The Virginian Pilot/Ledger Star* and *Navy Times.* Among his many awards: Leica Medal of Excellence Finalist, Atlanta Seminar on Photojournalism, Photographer of the Year, New Jersey Photographer of the Year, American Photographer's New Face in Photojournalism Finalist, numerous first-place awards from the New York Press Photographers

Association and an Excellence in Photojournalism award from Sigma Delta Chi. His work has been included in recent books such as *The African Americans* and *Songs of My People.*

SOMCHAI SATAYAPITAK

Thai/Bangkok
Somchai Satayapitak began his photographic career in Japan. In 1990, he founded 68 Studio Co., Ltd., his own studio in Thailand. His work includes magazine advertisements and beauty shots for magazine covers, household products and direct sales cosmetics companies. Khum Somchai also creates corporate executive portraits for both government and the private sector.

NAPAN SEVIKUL

Thai/Bangkok
Napan Sevikul has been a travel photographer and writer for over 20 years. Based in Thailand, he owns the audio-visual production house Bell Company, Ltd. He spends four to five months a year traveling the world promoting The Tourism Authority of Thailand as well as leading travel companies.

EMMANUEL SANTOS

Australian/Melbourne
A Filipino immigrant in Australia since 1982, Santos has produced photo essays and exhibitions on the human experience in China, Japan, India, the Philippines, Poland and Australia. His work has appeared in both Australian and worldwide publications. He has been working for a decade on a project on the lost tribes of Israel. He is a contributing photographer for Gamma Presse Images in Paris and a founding director of the M-33 Photo Agency in Melbourne.

MAGGIE STEBER

American/New York City
Steber won the Leica Medal of Excellence in 1987, First Prize for Spot News at the World Press Photo Competition in 1987, the Oliver Rebbot Award for Overseas coverage from Overseas Press Club, First Prize for News Documentary in the Pictures

of the Year competition in 1988, the Alicia Patterson Foundation Grant and the Ernst Haas Grant in 1988. Her book, *Dancing on Fire: Photographs from Haiti by Maggie Steber* was published by Aperture Books in 1992.

SCOTT THODE
American/New York City
Scott Thode's work has appeared in *Life, Newsweek, The Independent, Geo, Il Venerdi* and many other American and European publications. His work has been exhibited at the Visa Pour L'Image photo festival in Perpignon, France, in the Electric Blanket AIDS Project and at the P.S. 122 Gallery in New York City. In 1992, Thode was a finalist for the W. Eugene Smith Memorial Grant in Humanistic Photography. He won a first place at the Pictures of the Year competition sponsored by the National Press Photographers Association and took second place at the Gordon Parks Commemorative Photography Competition. Scott lives in New York City with his wife, Kathy Ryan, and their dog, Buster.

ALEX WEBB
American/New York City
Alex Webb was born in San Francisco. He has been working as a photojournalist since 1974 and joined Magnum Photos in 1976. His book of photographs from the tropics, *Hot Light/Half-Made Worlds*, was published in 1986, and another book about Haiti, *Under A Grudging Sun*, was published in 1989. He has exhibited widely in the United States and abroad in galleries and museums, including the Museum of Photographic Arts, the Walker Art Center, The Whitney Museum of American Art and the International Center of Photography. He has worked for numerous publications including *Life, Geo,* and *National Geographic*. He has received a New York Foundation for the Arts Grant and a National Education Association grant.

NIK WHEELER
British/Los Angeles
Nik Wheeler was born in Hitchin, England. He studied French and drama at Bristol University and French Civilization at the Sorbonne, Paris. Wheeler's world travels began in Athens, where he taught English. His photographic career began in Bangkok, where he co-published a guidebook to Thailand. In 1967, Wheeler moved to Vietnam as a combat photographer and joined United Press International during the 1968 Tet Offensive. He covered the 1970 Jordanian Civil War for *Time*, the October War for *Newsweek* and did assignments for *National Geographic* and *Paris Match*. Wheeler covered the fall of Saigon, the Montreal Olympics, the US presidential elections and the coronation of the King of Nepal. He now works from Los Angeles doing assignments for *National Geographic, GEO, International Wildlife* and travel magazines such as *Travel and Leisure, Travel Holiday, Islands* and *Departures*.

Wheeler's books include *Return to the Marshes* (1977), *Iraq—Land of Two Rivers* (1980), *This is China* (1981) and *Cloud Dwellers of the Himalayas* (1982). Since 1986, he has been co-publisher and principal photographer for the *Insider's Guides*. In addition to photography, he has written articles and columns for *Travel and Leisure, Islands* and *Aramco World*. In 1988, he was named Photographer of the Year by the Society of American Travel Writers.

NEVADA WIER
American/Santa Fe, New Mexico
Nevada Wier is a photographer specializing in remote corners of the globe, particularly Asia. She is a contract photographer with The Image Bank, and has been published in numerous national and international publications such as *Discovery, Smithsonian, Natural History, Popular Photography, Outside, Sawasdee, Photo Asia* and *Outdoor Photographer* among many others. She is a Fellow in the Explorers Club. Her most recent books are *The Land of Nine Dragons: Vietnam Today* (1992) and *Adventure Travel Photography* (1992). Weir is winner of the Lowell Thomas Best Travel Book of 1992 award.

MICHAEL S. YAMASHITA
American/Mendham, New Jersey
Photographer Mike Yamashita spends six months of the year on the road, shooting for a variety of editorial and commercial clients. He's been a regular contributor to *National Geographic* since 1979, covering such wide-ranging locations as China, Japan and Indonesia, Somalia and the Sudan, England and Ireland, New Guinea and New Jersey. He's also worked on over a dozen *National Geographic* books, including a year-long solo project, *Lakes, Peaks and Prairies*, shot along the entire U.S. and Canadian border. Yamashita most recently explored the mysteries of the Japanese garden, both in a feature for the *National Geographic* and in his latest book, *In the Japanese Garden*. His Japanese garden prints were exhibited at the National Galley of Art and are on permanent display at the Los Angeles Country Museum of Art. Yamashita has received awards from a variety of professional organizations including the National Press Photographers Pictures of the Year, the New York Art Directors Club, the Asian-American Journalists Association and the Pacific Area Travel Association. Yamashita has participated in three previous *Day in the Life* projects.

● Fish set out to dry in Songkhla. **EMMANUEL SANTOS**

A Day in the Life of Thailand Scrapbook

SHOOTING THE SHOOTERS
A Day in the Life of Thailand Co-Director James Marshall lines up the photographer's group portrait.
RICK BROWNE

THE MIRACLE WORKERS
(L-R) The *Day in the Life of Thailand* assignment team of Susy Barry, Khun Paiboon (Pat) Sonjai, Khun Wanchai Thavorntaveekul and Khun Addie Samerton worked around the clock.
RICK BROWNE

OPEN AIR STUDIO
Photographer, entrepreneur and raconteur extrordinaire, Patrick "Shrimp" Gauvain sets up shop at Three Pagodas Pass, near the Burmese border.
PATRICK "SHRIMP" GAUVAIN

EAST MEETS WEST
Hollywood photographer
Douglas Kirkland encounters
traditional Thai glamor.
RICK BROWNE

LEE-P OF FAITH
Kodak's Frances Lee flew
in from Rochester for A
Day in the Life of Thailand.
RICK BROWNE

THAI-ING ONE ON
(L-R) Kodak's Frances Lee,
Production Coordinator Barry
Sundermeier, Co-Director Rick
Browne, Francoise and Douglas
Kirkland, Co-Director James
Marshall, Logistics Coordina-
tor Linda Lamb and Project
Director David Cohen gather
at Bangkok's Lemon Grass
Restaurant.
RICK BROWNE

MAGNUM FORCE
(L-R) Magnum photographers Susan
Meiselas, Alex Webb, David Alan Harvey,
Abbas, Steve McCurry and Bruno Barbey.
ABBAS

WAT'S IT ALL ABOUT ?
Photographer Rick Rickman at Wat Benchamabohphit,
also known as the Marble Temple.
PAUL CHESLEY

215

A Day in the Life of Thailand Scrapbook

SECURITY ZONE
Loaded down with exposed film, *Day in the Life of Thailand* Production Coordinator Barry Sundermeier circumvents the X-ray machines at Narita Airport in Tokyo.
RICK BROWNE

ON A ROLL
Jim Sano of InnerAsia Expeditions collects film from Scott Thode and *The Miami Herald*'s Jeffery Allan Salter.
RICK BROWNE

IMPERIAL WELCOME
Day in the Life of Thailand photographers from around the world gathered at Bangkok's Imperial Queen's Park Hotel.
BARRY SUNDERMEIER

PICTURE THIS
Project Director David Cohen, holding a portrait of Their Majesties King Bhumibol and Queen Sirikit, is joined by project photographers and staff.
BARRY SUNDERMEIER

EASTERN EXPOSURE
Photographer Paul Chesley reloads at Bangkok's Wat Po.
PAUL CHESLEY

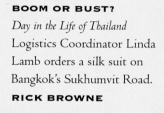

BOOM OR BUST?
Day in the Life of Thailand
Logistics Coordinator Linda
Lamb orders a silk suit on
Bangkok's Sukhumvit Road.
RICK BROWNE

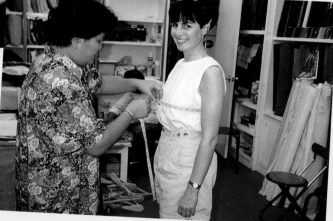

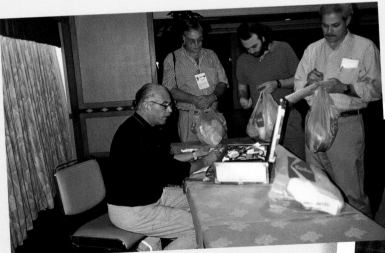

THE DOCTOR IS IN
Robert "Dr. Bob" Rabkin, MD dispenses
anti-malarial pills and other essentials to
Claus Meyer of Brazil, Baltimore's Steve
Rubin and Pulitzer Prize winner Larry
Price of Fort Worth, Texas.
RICK BROWNE

CZECH IT OUT!
Photographers Antonin Kratochvil of the Czech Republic
and Emmanuel Santos of the Philippines relaxing at a party
sponsored by the Tourism Authority of Thailand.
LINDA LAMB

Friends and Advisors

Joseph Abrams
Phra Acharn Vorasarn Chotithammo
Khun Akorn Hoontrakul
Rick Allen
Khun Amit Bose
Khun Amornrat Nutawat
Khun Amporn
Khun Anantaya Lekmark
The Angelo Family
Khun Apasara Thirawat
Khun Aprirak Kosayodhin
Khun Aree
Dr. Aree Jehsor
Hank Armstrong
Khun Arpa Akarasompope
The Aschermans
Som and Joseph Ashton
Khun Aurarat Saisorn
Diane Fuller Baldecchi
Monica Baltz
Khun Banthoon Lamsam
Kuhn Beat
The Bechelli's Gang
Catherine Bellanca
Janie Joseland Bennett
Khun Bhanu Maneevathanakul
The Bhayani Family
Carole Bidnick
Doug "Bix" Biederbecke
Rick Binger
Scott Bischoff
Susan Bloom
The Boyd Brothers
Dymphna Brennan
The Brenners

Rodd Buckle
John Bull
Richard Bush
Pam Byers
Robert Cameron
Woodfin Camp
Clayton Carlson
David Carriere
Robert Cave-Rogers
Mike Cerre
Ani Chamichian
Khun Chanasith Phaethanom
Jeanette Chapnick
Khun Chartchai Suwanasevok
Khun Chattan Kunjara Na Ayudhya
Khun Chawalit
Khun Chertchai Methanayanonda
Robert P. Childers II
Khun Chower Narulla
Dean Christon
Arta Christiansen
Dale and June Christiansen
Po Chung
Michael Claes
William Coblentz
Herb Cochran
Dan, Stacy and Big Andrew Cohen
Ellyn and Steven Cohen
Kara, Willie and Lucas Cohen
Norman & Hannah Cohen
The Collins Family
Jenny Collins
Michael Conkie
Lisa Cook
Guy Cooper

Edward J. Corcoran
Jackie, Paul, Aaron and Christopher
  Cornell
Caroline Cory
Joanna Cotler
George ("The Big Boss") Craig
Dennis, Barb and Andrew Crossen
Ross Cunningham
Cullen Curtiss
Carmine D'Aloisio
Peter Dam
Maura Carey Damacion
Khun Daranee Tanchaiswasd
Khun Dell
Keith Dellar
Ray and Barbara DeMoulin
Sophie Deprez
Marina Devoulin
Jurgen Dieter Voss
Anthea Disney
Walter Dodds
Sheila Donnelly
The Driskell Family
Julio C. Duque
Oscar Dystel
Lois and Mark Eagleton
Ray Eaton
Rachel Edilson
The Eisenbergs
John Englehart
The Epstein Family
Senator Diane Feinstein
The Feldman Family
Donna Ferrato
Linda Ferrer
Richard Fetzer
Mary Fiori
Maureen Flanagan
Timothy Fox
Rebecca Frazier
The Friend Family
David Friend
Julian J. L. Fryett
Dawn Fryling
Anabela Garth
Mathilde L. Genovese
Lou George
Ellen Georgiou
Carl Gibbs
Rudolph Gildemeister
Diego Goldberg
The Goldblum Family
John Goodman

John Goodyear
Monk Gordon
Tom Grady
Philip L. Graitcer, M.D.
The Grant Family
Steve Gregory
Elizabeth Grivas
Corina Guzman
Dave ("The Hag"), Emily & Casey
  Hagerman
Dr. Lynn Hamb
Quang Han
John Hancock
Keith Hardy
Brian Harries
Nick Harris
Audrey Hassler
Peter Hassler
Frank Hawke
Francois Hebel
Otilia and Vanessa Hernandez
Caroline Herter
The Higgins Family
James M. Highet
Carol A. Hilder
Maria Hjelm
Suzanne Hodgart
Sam Hoffman
The Holly Family
Mary Homi
Jerry Hopkins
Jim and Barbara Hurwitz
David Inocencio and Minette Siegel
Khun Israporn Posayanond
Jeff Jacobsen
Bob James
Gilbert Jardeleza
Khun Jintana Ratanawichaikul
Pensri Jitsittamon
John H. Johnson
Terry Johnson
Khun Jongjit Pisesrit
Margaret Kadoyama
Anna Kamdar
Mira and Alexander Kamdar
Pete Kamdar
Praveen and Caroline Kamdar
Vinuy and Chitra Kamdar
Khun Kamla Vacher-Ta
Khun Kamol Kruttharoj
The Kantola Family
Khun Katherine Sarasin
Shelley Katz

● In San Charoon, an Akha boy plays on a home-made cart. **LORI GRINKER**

Tom Keller
Kate Kelly and Bernard Ohanian
Khun Kentsara Kantaprom
Tony Kiernan
Carol M. Kim
Khun Kitiya Phomsadja
Khun Kittipong Prapattong
Judy and Sandy Kivowitz
The Kleiman Family
Khun Korrakot Houdkum
Ken Kragen
Michael J. Kressbach
Jeff Kriendler
Bob Kuhn
Tom Kunhardt
Susan Kunze
Dr. Joseph Kushner
Eliane and Jean Pierre Laffont
Mr. and Mrs. Stuart Lamb
Stuart M. Lamb, Jr.
Bao Lamsam
Nathaniel Lande
Alex Lanham
Frances Lee
Wendy Lee
John Leicester
Richard and Sharon Levick
The Levinson Family
Khun Li Dan
Lee, Josh, Cassie and Bez Liberman
Bertil Lintner
The Lloyd Family
Michael G. Loew
Paul Logan
Jared Long
Barbara Loren
Russ Lowe
Leonard Lueras
Sunny Lyrek
Peter Macchia
Andy MacInnes and Kathy Fong
Diana and John Mack
Chuck Maffia
George Mann
Brenda Marsh
Heather Marshall
Nathan Marshall
Aki Matsuura
The McAlpin Family
The McCandless-Belt Family
H. E. John McCarthy
The McKiernan Family
The McLaughlin Family

● On the Royal Railway Golf Course in Bangkok. **PASSAKORN PAVILAI**

Michelle McNally
Khun Meechai
Father Joseph Meier
Saun Mekwai
The Menuez Family
Charlene Mercadante
Pedro Meyer and Trisha Ziff
Didier Millet
Jonathan Mills
Tom Mintier
Ida Mintz
John Moffly
Toby Momtaz
The Monetta Family
Genevieve Morgan

Louie Morales
Khun Myke
Khun Nalinee Bunnag
Khun Napaporn Satayalai
Khun Narisara Lauhakamin
Khun Narissa Yingcharoen
Khun Narong Chivangkur
Khun Narong Intanate
Khun Nattakarn Jaicompang
Matthew Naythons, M.D.
Khun Nid
Khun Nirandorn Mekbot
Khun Noppadol Lertussavavivat
Lisa Nordhoff
Cheryl and Allen Nugent

Khun Oithip Nitiyanant
Khun Orawan Intratat
Khun Orawan Jai-A
Brian O'Reilly
Dan Oshema
Edward Outlaw
John Owen
Khun Pakhawat Kovithvathanaphong
Khun Panida Hirunpornisit
Khun Panrapee Roekchamnong
Nathalie Paque
Evelynne Thambie Pasimio
Khun Patcharawalai Phanthwong
Michael Pazdon
Sara Pearl
The Pedersen Family
Khun Penpun Visuddhi Na Ayudhya
Gabe and Pat Perle
Liz Perle and Steve and David
  McKenna
The Peters Family
Richard L. Peters
Jennifer Petersen
Steve Peterson
Jim Pfeiffer
Khun Phan Wannamethee
Khun Phongthawat Phuangkanok
Khun Piya Wechasethanon
Robert Pledge
Khun Pongsit S. Veerapong
Khun Pornpimol Kanthatham
Khun Pornsri Luphaiboon
Khun Praesert Lipiwathana
Khun Prapansak Bhatyanond
Kru Prateep
Khun Premsiri Nimitmongkol
Khun Prowphun Vongsawatdicat
Khun Puripat Pakavaleetorn
Frank Gordon-Quiroga
Paulann Rabkin
Khun Rachan Namwat
Michael Rand
Khun Ratanawalee Loharjun
Khun Rawewan Prakobpol
James Reed
Patti Richards
Michelle Ried
The Rieser Family
The Riklin Family
Anne Rogers
Noah Rosen
The Rosenberg Family
John Rothmann

FRIENDS AND ADVISORS

Khun Royston Minjoo
Jacqueline Rudasics
Khun Runjene Raghavan
Chris Ryan
Kathy Ryan
Prof. Scott Sagan
Khun Samran Kaewsrengam and
Family
Curt Sanburn
Khun Sangthong Thimthae
Khun Sanphasit Koompraphant
Khun Saravut Vacharapol
Khun Sareelak Pukham-anan
Ron Savir
Dr. Leonard and Millie Schwartz
Dave Scypinski
Rob Scypinski
Thomas A. Seale
Khun Seangsuree Pengyot
Doug Seator
Khun Seree Wangpaichitr
Barry Shea
The Sherman Family
Stephanie Sherman
Wendell J. Sims
Khun Siroj Mingkwun
Khun Sivaporn Benjaphureerat
Whitney Small
Wayman F. Smith III
Khun Somchai Sutikulphanit
Khun Somnuk Nuntachaibuncha
Reverand Sompong Umbuar
Pat Steenrod
The Steinberg Family
Michelle Stephenson
Teri Stewart
John Clay and Charlotte Stites
Dr. Sucharti Sungkasem
Khun Sudhasinee Vajrabul
Khun Sumoin Krisanamitra
Khun Sumonta Nakornthab
John and Pauline Sundermeier
Khun Supachitra Dhanarajata
Khun Supakorn Yamsuk
Khun Supatana Atorn-Phtai
Khun Suphot Hudakorn
Khun Surachai Nikrothanont
Dr. Suraphol Virulrak
Khun Surapong Chookijkul
Khun Surin Krittayaphongphun
Lena Tabori
The Taylor Family
Khun Teerasak Pongsawat

● Island in the Andaman Sea. **NAPAN SEVIKUL**

Khun Thanpuying Mom Luang
Nualpong Senanarong
Khun Thitasak
Jordan Thorn
Margot Towie
Frank Trapper
Khun Tuenjai Jiarathanakul
Edith Turner
Sally Tuttolomondo
Khun Twitath Warintrakom
Michael Udelson
Khun Udomsak Pansupa
Mark A. M. Van Ogtrop
Ignacio Vasallo
Drew Vella
Khun Venai Phisutsinthop
Khun Vinai Suttharoj

Khun Vorayoot Meksute
Colin Wade
Gary Wakahiro
Keri Walker
Khun Wanchai Thavornthaveekul
Khun Wanna Sae-Chua
Charles Ward
Khun Wasana Nathmontri
Khun Wat
Thomas D. Watson
Khun Weerawudht and Khun
Sumontip Otrakul
Sharon Weiner
Kevin Weldon
Michael Wellman
Amy Wels
Janie Westenfeder

Eric and Janet Weyenberg
Evelyn White
Ed Wieger
Khun Wilasinee Katanoi
Jill Williams-Gilmore
Curtis Willocks
Beau Wilson
Khun Wineenart Phanvut
Khun Witchitra Watcharawaratorn
Khun Wittaya Wongwanich
Khun Worasumon and Khun
Worathip Otrakul
Khun Yingsak
Khun Youkonton Ratarasarn
Betsy Young
Khun Yuki

ORGANIZATIONS

American Chamber of Commerce
in Thailand
Ban Kan Ta Kwian Elementary School
BWC Chrome Labs
Chulalongkorn University
Citibank
Compuprint
Foreign Correspondents Club
of Thailand
Haskin Press
Hi-Fi
The San Francisco Hilton
Joseph Mutti Travel, SF
Khong Chia Police Station
Kinko's
Light Waves
The Manager Company
Marina Super
The Media Vault
Modern Effects
The New Lab
Presko Limited
Thairath Newspaper
Thamkrabok Buddhist Monk
Sanctuary
Tour East (Thailand) Limited
Tourism Authority of Thailand
U.S. & Foreign Commercial Service/
United States Embassy
The Value Systems Co., Ltd.
Wat Sra Kaew Temple
The Yellow Leaf People

A Day in the Life of Thailand
Selected Bibliography

"California Company to Produce 5,900 Electric 3-Wheeled Taxis for Thailand." *Alternative Energy Network Online Today* (May 10, 1994).

Cooper, Robert & Nanthapa. *Culture Shock! Thailand*. Singapore: Times Editions Pte. Ltd., 1990.

Corben, Ron. "Thailand: Blistering Growth May Lead To Overheating." Inter Press Service (Dec. 15, 1993), Global Information Network.

Cumming-Bruce, Nicholas. "A life of war and waiting." *U.S. News & World Report* (Oct. 23, 1989): 44-45.

Cummings, Joe. *Thailand*. Singapore: Lonely Planet Publications, 1992.

Davies, Ben. *Thailand*. Chicago: Passport Books, 1993.

Ekachai, Sanitsuda. *Behind the Smile*. Bangkok: The Post Publishing Co., Ltd., 1991.

Exploring Thailand. New York: Fodor's Travel Publications, Inc., 1993.

Hilltribes of Thailand. Bangkok: Pacific Rim Press (HK) Co. Ltd., 1992.

Horn, Robert. "A dream with a kick to it." *Sports Illustrated* (November 1990): 132-134.

Horn, Robert. "Tee time for traders." *Sports Illustrated* (September 1991): 77.

Hoskin, John. *A Guide to Bangkok*. Bangkok: Asia Books, 1992.

Hoskin, John. *A Guide to Thailand*. Bangkok: Asia Books, 1992.

"Jam today, bigger jam tomorrow." *The Economist* (July 6, 1991): 38.

Kasetsiri, Charnvit, *The Rise of Ayudhya*. Kuala Lumpur: Oxford University Press, 1976.

Let's Go: Thailand. Cambridge, Mass.: Harvard Student Agencies, 1994.

"Natural rubber in Thailand." *Rubber Trends* (Summer 1993): 33-40.

Neff, Craig; Sullivan, Robert. "The widest world of sports." *Sports Illustrated* (April 1986): 22.

Parkes, Carl. *Thailand Handbook*. Chico, Calif.: Moon Publications, 1992.

Ransdell, Eric. "Bridge on the River Kwai." *U.S. News & World Report* (December 3, 1990) : 14.

"Rice and fall." *The Economist* (June 19, 1993): 35-36.

Roscoe, Gerald. *The Buddha's Life*. Bangkok: Pacific Rim Press, 1992.

Roscoe, Gerald. *The Good Life*. Bangkok: Pacific Rim Press, 1992.

Shaw, David. "Thais, Malaysians plan research." *European Rubber Journal* (January 1992): 8-9.

Sivaraman, Satyanarayan. "Thailand-Religion." Inter Press Service (Feb. 16, 1994), Global Information Network.

Sivaraman, Satyanarayan. "Thailand: Settled Sea Gypsies May Be on the Move Again." Inter Press Service (February 18, 1994), Global Information Network.

"Snarl-up: Thailand." *The Economist* (Sept. 4, 1993): 36-37.

Sullivan, Deidre. "Software Alliance sells system to bank in Thailand." *American Banker* (June 24, 1994): 17.

Swift, E.M. "Sport in the land of Sanuk." *Sports Illustrated* (February 1988): 112-121.

Tettoni, Luca Invernizzi. *A Guide to Chiang Mai and Northern Thailand*. Bangkok: Asia Books, 1992.

Tomsen, Peter. "Cambodia: recent developments (transcript)." *U.S. Department of State Dispatch* (May 23, 1994): 343-344.

Thailand. Boston: Houghton Mifflin Company, 1993.

"Thailand: A fast-growing market, but for what kinds of consumer goods?" *Market Asia Pacific* (October 15, 1993).

Thailand, Indochina and Burma Handbook. Chicago: Passport Books, 1993.

Thailand in the '90s. Thailand: The Office of the Prime Minister, Royal Thai Government, 1991.

"The mall, the merrier." *The Economist* (August 27, 1994): 59.

"Who's Nicest?" *The Economist* (August 13, 1994): 31-32.

Warren, William. *Bangkok's Waterways*. Bangkok: R. Ian Lloyd Productions Pte. Ltd., 1989.

Wyatt, David K. *Thailand: A Short History*. New Haven: Yale University Press, 1984.

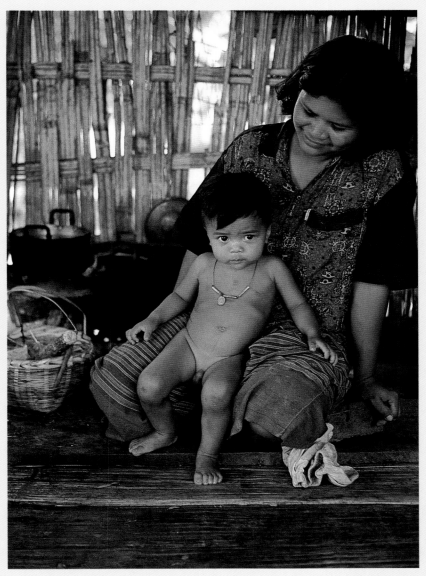

● A grandmother and child in the village of Ban Kan Ta Kwian. **HIROJI KUBOTA**

A Day in the Life of Thailand Sponsors

This project was made possible by:

THAI FARMERS BANK PUBLIC COMPANY LIMITED

Proud of achieving half a century of banking excellence, Thai Farmers Bank Public Company Limited looks forward to the next 50 years with great excitement and determination.

In view of the effects of globalization and liberalization in the Thai financial service industry in the next century, Thai Farmers Bank has launched a program of fundamental change in its effort to bring world-class banking services to Thailand.

Thai Farmers Bank has invested in some of the world's most advanced technology and applied it to every part of the bank's business to make many of these changes possible.

Even more remarkable have been the changes within Thai Farmers Bank's people, each of whom have embraced these transitions or become the catalyst in the bank's quest for constant improvement. It is their "Spirit of Excellence" that is making change a reality.

The results of the ongoing process are evident in Thai Farmers Bank's move to the forefront in Thailand's capital markets, in an expanding presence throughout the region, and, very dramatically, in its newly redesigned branches nationwide.

Whether it's public offering of capital market instruments or the opening of an individual checking account, Thai Farmers Bank's goal is to provide all customers—from the large enterprise to the small individual consumer—with the information they need and the speed and expertise of service they demand.

The same "Spirit of Excellence" unfolds further as Thai Farmers Bank prepares to locate to a newer and bigger head office—a 42-story landmark building at the foot of the Rama IX bridge.

On the wings of its "Spirit of Excellence," the Thai Farmers Bank's mission continues—that is, not only to build its own future, but also to help build Thailand's future.

Additional sponsorship provided by:

SECURITIES ONE PUBLIC COMPANY LIMITED

Securities One Public Company Limited is proud to be a part of *A Day in the Life of Thailand*. Securities One is Thailand's leading securities brokerage company. It holds licenses in Securities Brokerage, Securities Trading, Investment Advisory and Securities Registrar Service. Securities One was established on March 7, 1975, and the company's registered capital has since increased to 1,082 million baht. Securities One has won the confidence of a large and growing number of clientele, thus elevating the company to the top securities company in total annual trading volume in 1993. Securities One was also proud to maintain the largest trading volume in 1994.

The company's Research Institute conducts professional research and analysis conscientiously in the spirit of our corporate slogan: "Firm in Principle, First in Securities."

Securities One is also one of the most active Thai securities firms in providing corporate finance services, which include financial structuring, corporate restructure and the listing of companies on the Stock Exchange, from preparatory stages through the mandatory two year post-listing performance monitoring. Based on those issues in which the company has played a key role in public offerings during the past three years, 1992-94, Securities One is one of the most active securities firms in the industry.

Securities Registrar Service is another of our services, offering share registration services to limited companies, both listed and unlisted in the Stock Exchange of Thailand. The scope of services includes share registration, share transfer, share certificate issuance, dividend payment, capital increase projects and other related shareholders services.

Presently, Securities One has nine provincial sales offices in the upcountry of Thailand, and also plans to open three branches in Bangkok in 1995.

THE IMPERIAL QUEEN'S PARK HOTEL

For more than 20 years, the Imperial Family of Hotels has been at the forefront of Thailand's dynamic tourism industry, creating a network of international quality hotels in destinations of unique and breathtaking appeal.

The family, such an important element in the traditional Thai way of life, is therefore an entirely appropriate symbol for all of our hotels. It is a theme which embraces everything we do, from the close relations we enjoy with our staff to the welcome we offer all our guests.

To stay with us is to experience the very essence of one of the world's most beautiful countries.

Having the opportunity to participate in *A Day in the Life of Thailand* is extremely gratifying for The Imperial Family of Hotels. It is the celebration of a nation which we, as a Thai company, wholeheartedly support.

Mr. Akorn Hoontrakul, Chairman
The Imperial Family of Hotels

EASTMAN KODAK COMPANY

Eastman Kodak Company, the world leader in photography, produces films, papers and chemicals for professional and amateur use; electronic imaging products; motion picture films; copier-duplicators; and hundreds of other products for business and industry, health care and the home. The company employs more than 110,000 people worldwide, 57,000 of them in the US. In 1993, Kodak revenues totaled more than $16.4 billion, with nearly half coming from sales outside the US.

SERM SUK PUBLIC COMPANY LTD.

PEPSI-COLA (THAI) TRADING CO., LTD.

Pepsi honors the Golden Jubilee of His Majesty the King's accession to the throne. In common with the Thai people, we acknowledge His Majesty's special contribution to promoting harmony and unity throughout the Kingdom.

The King's Golden Jubilee is also an opportune time to reflect on his leadership role in fostering awareness of the environment. In recent times this has focused on water quality and conservation.

For more than 40 years, Pepsi has been part of the fabric of Thai society—from Bangkok's surging business pulse to the provincial cities and marine and rural hinterlands. Through this close interaction, fostered by many types of community support, Pepsi has become widely acknowledged as the preferred soft drink choice.

This year one of our major community involvements will lie in promoting water quality and conservation in association with the Thai

National Youth Bureau. In so doing, Pepsi recognizes that water is not only a precious resource—it is close to the hearts and minds of all Thai people, symbolized by the mighty Chao Phrya and a myriad of other waterways.

Pepsi joins hands with the people of Thailand in promoting measures designed to protect this key resource and in honoring the example of His Majesty.

TOURISM AUTHORITY OF THAILAND

Ever since its founding in 1960, the Tourism Authority of Thailand (TAT) has been instrumental in fostering the growth of the Thai tourism industry. From a country that had only 81,340 foreign tourist arrivals three decades ago, Thailand welcomed over 6 million overseas tourists in 1994. TAT expects this total to jump to 6.7 million and 7.2 million in 1995 and 1996, respectively. TAT, as the national tourist organization, has been involved in almost all aspects of the country's tourism promotion and development. Through its 22 domestic and 17

overseas offices, TAT supports the work of the private sector by undertaking marketing activities aimed at increasing travel to and inside Thailand. TAT consistently promotes Thailand, its attractions and destinations through high-profile printed and television advertising and active participation in travel trade shows worldwide.

On the development side, TAT has been planning, surveying and studying tourist destination development to set trends for related organizations to follow, especially various basic necessities in tourism. Furthermore, TAT supports tourism resources conservation in local areas, and conservation of Thai culture and traditions to attract tourists. TAT also supports and encourages local areas to produce folk arts and crafts in demand by tourists as souvenirs.

To provide safety to tourists traveling in the country, TAT works closely with the Tourist Police and has its own Tourist Assistance Center to help tourists with various matters.

TAT is committed to sustainable and long-term tourism development. Thailand's unique and delicate nature and culture are the country's most valuable tourism

resources, and TAT works closely with all offices concerned to ensure that visitors and future generations of Thais can continue to enjoy them in coming years.

THAI AIRWAYS INTERNATIONAL

Thai Airways International, the national carrier of the Kingdom of Thailand, is one of the most successful airlines in the world today.

Established in 1960, Thai presently operates a fleet of over 65 of the latest jets to more than 70 worldwide destinations across 35 countries— including over 20 destinations around Thailand.

With the introduction of new equipment such as the Airbus A330, and the Boeing 777 which is currently on order, Thai's fleet remains one of the youngest in Asia, with an average age of approximately six years per aircraft.

The total number of passengers carried by Thai has grown year after year throughout its 34-year history. Thai achieved this enviable growth record partly through pioneering new destinations, such as Kathmandu and Bali, and also through product innovation, being, for example, the first Asian airline to introduce Business Class.

Massive capital and manpower resource deployment enables Thai to be virtually self-sufficient in most aspects of operation, including such vital functions as aircraft maintenance, catering and cargo.

With its home base at Bangkok's Don Maung airport, Thai is positioned at the most popular and central gateway to Asia and Indochina.

Thai International is Thailand's largest public corporation. With

almost 20,000 staff and 170,000 shareholders, the company is virtually unequaled within the airline industry in having earned profits for each of the last 29 years.

Thai Airways International is proud to sponsor *A Day in the Life of Thailand.*

INNERASIA EXPEDITIONS, SAN FRANCISCO

InnerAsia Expeditions, San Francisco, is a professional travel management corporation providing a broad range of travel and location management services for corporations, individuals and travel agents, as well as marketing support for corporations and government tourism offices. The company specializes in remote locations and complicated logistical situations. It has operations throughout Asia, Central and South America, Africa, Europe and the Pacific

● Soccer fans at Yubharaj College in Chiang Mai. **ROBIN MOYER**

In Nong Khai, on the Laotian border,
worshippers place candles on the
boundary wall of Wat Phochai.
CAROL GUZY